THE
PASSIONATE
JOURNEY

MARTY A. BULLIS

Regal

From Gospel Light
Ventura, California, U.S.A.

PUBLISHED BY REGAL BOOKS
FROM GOSPEL LIGHT
VENTURA, CALIFORNIA, U.S.A.
PRINTED IN THE U.S.A.

For a free catalog of resources from Regal Books/Gospel Light, please call your Christian supplier or contact us at 1-800-4-GOSPEL *or* www.regalbooks.com.

All Scripture quotations are taken from the following sources:

The Message—Scripture taken from *The Message*. Copyright © by Eugene H. Peterson, 1993, 1994, 1995. Used by permission of NavPress Publishing Group.
NRSV—The Scripture quotations contained herein are from the *New Revised Standard Version Bible,* copyright 1989, by the Division of Christian Education of the National Council of the Churches of Christ in the U.S.A. Used by permission. All rights reserved.
RSV—From the *Revised Standard Version* of the Bible, copyright 1946, 1952, and 1971 by the Division of Christian Education of the National Council of the Churches of Christ in the U.S.A. Used by permission.

Library of Congress Cataloging-in-Publication Data
Bullis, Marty A.
  The passionate journey / Marty Bullis.
      p. cm.
  Includes bibliographical references.
  ISBN 0-8307-4318-9 (hard cover) — ISBN 0-8307-4392-8 (international trade paper)
  1. Lent—Meditations. 2. Easter—Meditations. 3. Bible. N.T. Gospels—Devotional use.
I. Title.
  BV85.B78 2006
  242'.34—dc22   2006033135

1   2   3   4   5   6   7   8   9   10   /   10   09   08   07

Rights for publishing this book in other languages are contracted by Gospel Light Worldwide, the international nonprofit ministry of Gospel Light. Gospel Light Worldwide also provides publishing and technical assistance to international publishers dedicated to producing Sunday School and Vacation Bible School curricula and books in the languages of the world. For additional information, visit www.gospellightworldwide.org; write to Gospel Light Worldwide, P.O. Box 3875, Ventura, CA 93006; or send an e-mail to info@gospellightworldwide.org.

CONTENTS

Lent is a gift that is extensively observed by many Christians but also extensively underappreciated by many. Ignorance accounts for much of the underappreciation—some of us have simply never heard of it, or having heard of it never paid much attention to it. Impatience accounts for the rest—we let the non-worshiping world tell us how to spend our time, mostly in "getting and spending." We impatiently shrug off the wise counsel that has permeated most of the centuries of the Church's life—counsel that directs us to deliberately take 40 days every spring to reorient our lives by using the compass of Jesus' death and resurrection. We ignore the gift of time because we "don't have time."

But once we understand, and take a long and loving look at the gift, any and all excuses seem trivial. This time-gift allows us ample time each year to escape from the jerky, helter-skelter Saint Vitus's dance of instant gratification and mindless distraction that is piped 24 hours a day by the devil. It provides time-conditions sufficient to recover the deep rhythms of meditative prayer that can be assimilated into our daily work as unhurried melodic obedience and praise.

The Church's 40-day gift of time to Christian men and women is woven into the story of Jesus' journey to the cross. But the number 40 is not arbitrary. Forty is a number associated biblically with deeply formed transitions: Forty years for Moses in the wilderness to get Egypt out of his spirit and get ready for an Exodus life. Forty days for Elijah to get Jezebel out of his spirit and get ready for a fresh encounter with God at Sinai. And 40 days for us every year to get detoxed from the consumer addictions of American culture.

One of the serious disabilities that cripples the men and women who follow Jesus on American roads is our unthinking but stubborn individualism. We grow up thinking that we do the Christian thing best when we do it alone, without interference, without traditions. We are willing to gather with others for worship on Sundays, sometimes join a study group, and help out in missions projects. But for really serious matters, we insist on taking things in regard to God and our souls into our own hands. This, despite the frequent and unqualified revelation of Scripture and church experience that we are each of us a member of the Body of Christ, that we are relational beings to the core, that our highest calling is to receive and give love—transactions that require relationship with others. And not least, the fact that God is revealed to us as emphatically relational—three times personal as Trinity—who can only be known relationally as He is in Himself—in a community of persons.

The time-gift of Lent is a gift of the Holy Spirit to the community of men and women who intend to follow Jesus. The gift is personal, but it is not private—we can't take and do with it what we like; others are necessarily involved. So not only are we provided with these 40 days to recover rhythms of grace, but we are also provided the gift of companions for deepening our personal relationships with one another on the journey.

One thing more: Our guide on this Lenten journey, Dr. Marty Bullis, uses words in this context—meditative and prayerful words—as well as anyone I know and far better than most. There is not a hint of devotional saccharine in these pages, not a dishonest sentence. He keeps our attention on the clean, austere, soul-penetrating life of Jesus to make sure that we don't squander a single day of this lavish time-gift of Lent.

Eugene H. Peterson
Professor Emeritus of Spiritual Theology
Regent College
Vancouver, B.C.

DEDICATION

For Tracie
who helps me see Jesus in the darkness

ACKNOWLEDGMENTS

No task we undertake in our Christian lives is done in isolation. The Body of Christ—the community of saints—at all times pervades our living, even should we seem to be alone. Fellow believers are there—sometimes close by, sometimes on the margins—praying faithfully, worshiping zestfully and loving passionately. As I worked alone in my office writing this text, I was supported by a host of wonderful people.

My wife, Tracie, and my children, Ryker and Madelen, are the kind of people you want to be on a journey with. They're fun, beautiful and full of life. They keep me going on my darkest days and dance with me on my lightest. This book is full of their inspiration.

My parents, Bill and Madeline Bullis, are both gifted teachers who have guided my writing since the days when I was learning to hold a pencil properly.

What a marvelous blessing it is to have friends in Christ! Eugene and Jan Peterson show me how to stick at this faith for the long haul—this long obedience of ours. George and Ann Pace, godparents extraordinaire, provide the kind of insight and perspective a king should hope for.

I was very fortunate to have a Lenten community of faith that read these devotions as they were being written. Pat Bruce and Lee Morrison are thoughtful and inspiring mentors—the kind of people I want to be around! Paula Caldwell shared her gift of encouragement with me after reading an early draft. Bill and Carol Moore have kept me in daily prayer and offered valuable editing suggestions. The Lenten Group at First Presbyterian Church of Philipsburg, Pennsylvania, (Jeff and Mary Beth Eyet, Mary Gilham, Darrell and Helen Hollis, Dick and Holly Kithcart, and Dottie Isaacson) helped me understand how this material would work in a group setting. Thanks to you all!

As a writer, I am blessed to have a number of professionals who support my work. Janet Benrey is a superb literary agent who not only loves words but also prayerfully attends to business matters. My editor at Regal Books, Deena Davis, took such care with my prose that she blessed my socks off. Kim Bangs, the author relations manager at Regal, juggles a philosopher's questions with grace and speed. And thanks to the support staff at Regal for their faithful work in God's kingdom.

Finally, thanks to you, the reader, for entering into this Lenten journey with saints all around the world. May God lead you into the darkness toward the light of Easter.

The 40 days of Lent are an inversion of the spirit. A topsy-turvy jumbling of the Christian's psyche. For as the world moves out of winter with a lightening of the sky and warming of the atmosphere, the Christian walks into the darkness—into the chilling death of Jesus. It is a death march forced upon us each year in which the self is called to die, giving itself over to the will of God.

The journey is made increasingly difficult by a world that prizes the mechanisms and machinery of self-fulfillment. It is an age where light shines any time of the day, where minds are entertained to overflowing at the push of a button, where sweet drinks and delicious treats drop from dispensers. "Surfeit" and "satiety" are the definitive terms, not "sacrifice" and "restriction." Asking the self to die a little each day for six weeks is a countercultural act—an act of resistance against the circling powers. It is the Christian equivalent of *raging against the machine*—subversion of society and transformation of the person balled into one observance.

It is good to understand this as you begin the journey. Flowers will begin to bloom. But for you they'll be a reminder of a death and burial. People around you will start their spring fitness regimens, working off their winter bulges, strengthening their resolve. For you there'll be relinquishment, confinement and giving over your self-resolve to something much higher—the hand of God at work within. You will see people jumpstarting, pepping and reviving themselves. You will be dying. You'll be in forced waiting, emptying the garbage while others fill their houses. You're in for a hard time. So what's the good news? This is just what you need, just what your self needs.

Lent is a journey of remembrance. Your journey starts in your memory. The pilgrim must know the story of Jesus, but not get in its way. She or he must let the Spirit of God reveal the story's meaning in the present. So, we will read again the Scripture pertaining to Christ's death march. We will mull them and chew on them while they eat away our pretensions. This is the spirit of resistance that our society needs—resistance to the self. Here, we are at the heart of the battle for goodness—center ring in the fight against the world's ills.

There's a funny thing about this journey for Christians: It must be a communal act. At the same time that we're subverting our society, we're building community. There is no holing ourselves within a cave, no solitary "getting right with God." Such an approach is not possible for the Christian. In fact, it would be counter to God's will. We'd be "spiritual cowboys" if we were to take this approach—jacking our self up by its bootstraps. The early Desert Fathers and Mothers, the Abbas and Ammas of the Egyptian desert knew this. Withdrawal into the caves of the desert was not for them withdrawal from community, but an act of focusing God's energies for the sake of the community. We'll have many periods of solitude during Lent, but solitude infused with community. For the sake of Jesus' body, we die each day. Hands, hearts, feet, stomachs, bottoms, intestines. Members of Christ's body restored through death. Proper function replacing cancerous self-attention.

Some of us will walk through Lent with persons we've known for many years, in churches where we've grown up and grown old. Others of us will walk with people who we're still learning to live with. Sadly for the self, but happily for Christ, we cannot choose the participants in this pilgrimage, cannot choose the members of the Body of Christ. They are Christ's pilgrims, not ours. We'll be walking toward the cross with some people our selves cannot stand. It is good then to remember Christ's commands of "die to self" and "Whoever does not carry the cross and follow me cannot be my disciple" (Luke 14:27, *NRSV*). Remember, your death march is with others, but it is also *for* them.

———

What follows are daily Scripture readings for the Lenten season accompanied by short reflections, bidding prayers and space for journaling. Start by reading the Scripture passage for the day. (Due to space considerations, only a brief excerpt of the daily Gospel reading is printed with each devotion. Have your Bible handy so that you can read the full passage.) Pause and meditate on parts of the Scripture that strike you. Next, read the accompanying reflection that focuses on an aspect of the Gospel passage. Following the reflection, set aside a few minutes for prayer as you open your heart to God. A four-part bidding prayer is provided to guide you. Rest in silence for a short time at the end of each line of prayer. The final prayer asks God to enliven your spirit as you write your thoughts to Him during the time of journaling. This fourfold structure (Scripture, reflection, prayer and journaling) moves us from hearing God's Word to receiving this Word in our spirit and then responding to this Word in prayer and action.

There are 41 devotions—40 for the days from Ash Wednesday to Holy Saturday (excluding Sundays) and one for Easter. The devotions begin with Christ's anointing at Bethany and follow the Passion story through Christ's burial. Daily Scripture readings from the Gospels are offered in a fairly chronological order.

Sundays are not counted as part of the Lenten observance— Sunday being the day of Christ's resurrection. The Church continues to celebrate Christ's resurrection, even as it is observing His death. On the six Sundays that fall during the Lenten journey, short Scripture readings from the resurrection story are provided along with reflections and bidding prayers; however, in observance of the Sabbath day of rest, no journaling space is provided.

The devotional is well suited for use by small groups that meet during Lent. A "Lenten Litany for Small Groups" is included as a guide for structuring group meetings. The litany includes responsive readings and time for discussion and silent reflection.

———

"Remember, you are dust and to dust you shall return!"
Words for the imposition of ashes—Ash Wednesday

PART ONE

THE FIRST 10 DAYS

*A woman came to [Jesus] with an alabaster jar of very costly ointment,
and she poured it on his head as he sat at the table. . . . [Jesus said,]
"By pouring this ointment on my body she has prepared me for burial."*

Matthew 26:7,12, *NRSV*

THE GOSPEL READING
Matthew 26:1-13, *NRSV*

THE REFLECTION
DEATH PREPARATIONS

14

We begin our journey with an unusual anointing. Today Christians enter churches around the world in quiet reflection and exit with a death mark upon their foreheads—ashes mixed with oil applied in the shape of a cross. Reminders of the death of our Lord, and our deaths. I speak in the plural, highlighting the two types of human death we contemplate during Lent. There is the daily death of self (our quotidian struggle to give over all those parts of our being that are resisting God) that we attend to with renewed vigor during Lent. Then there is the future death of our physical body, which the ashes remind us is looming. While death of self marks growth in Christ, physical death underscores the fate of this world—destruction. Our hope is that as we move toward our physical end through processes of decay, we grow in new life with Christ by giving up our preoccupation with self. We would like to see our power in these arenas be inversely proportional—less able to stop the decay of our body, more empowered to let our self die for the sake of Christ.

The Scripture reading recounts an anointing prior to Christ's death. Our Lord tells His disciples that it is preparation for burial. Some of those around Him do not understand the act. They even ridicule it. In a few days, Jesus gives up His body and His will to the will of the Father. We remember His words: "Father, if thou art willing, remove this cup from me; nevertheless, not my will, but thine, be done" (Luke 22:42, *RSV*). Like Christ, you are preparing for death. Receiving a symbol upon your body that others will not understand. Walking toward acts of renunciation that confuse them. It is the beginning of your death march—death of self during Lent. But it also marks growth in Christ—growing strength to be filled with God's will.

Powers continue to exist that would arrest our growth and kill us even as our Lord was arrested and killed. These are the enemies of God's economy. These forces would steal what is true in us, having us glorify rebellious desires and ignore those people around us whom God would have us help.

As you encounter difficulties in the next few weeks, let your breath prayer be the words of Christ, "Not my will, but thine be done." Just as the powers of evil misjudged God's work in Christ, so too they will misjudge what God is able to do within your life.

THE BIDDING PRAYER

Help me, Lord Jesus, die to self this day. (silence)
Light of the world, shine into my darkness. (silence)
Jesus, show me how to serve the members of Your Body. (silence)
Enliven my spirit as I reveal myself to You in written word. (silence)

THE JOURNAL

Then Judas Iscariot, who was one of the twelve, went to the chief priests in order to betray him to them. When they heard it, they were greatly pleased, and promised to give him money. So he began to look for an opportunity to betray him.

Mark 14:10-11, *NRSV*

THE GOSPEL READING
Mark 14:10-11, *NRSV*

THE REFLECTION
TURNING AWAY

18

The first overt act of turning away in Mark's account of Christ's Passion belongs to Judas. Here is betrayal full-blown, the friend-become-enemy seeking the destruction of one he once loved. So many mental disappointments must have occurred within Judas before this point. We're given much too little background on his journey to evil to speculate coherently. And anyway, Judas's *psyche* is not central to the story Mark wants to tell.

Judas's *actions* take center stage in this drama. Mark shines the spotlight on "going" and "looking." Betrayal finds feet and eyes willing to work. Like a negative image, Judas's actions stand against Christ's. A few days after this visit by Judas to the chief priests, he exits the Last Supper to set the trap for Jesus. Christ turns to the remaining disciples and in the middle of His farewell discourse says, "No one has greater love than this, to lay down one's life for one's friends" (John 15:13, *NRSV*). They are words that Judas cannot hear—not with his ears, not with his soul. Judas is moving to kill his friends; Christ is moving to die for His. Our reaction as we read the story is visceral. Disgust forms in our gut.

Death of the self is the defining act of Christ's life. It is an act that Judas cannot perform. John's Gospel attempts to soften our disgust by explaining that Judas was greedy. John's account of Christ's anointing at Bethany adds these words of Judas and a comment from John: "'Why was this perfume not sold for three hundred denarii and the money given to the poor?' (He said this not because he cared for the poor, but because he was a thief; he kept the common purse and used to steal what was put into it)" (John 12:5-6, *NRSV*). We feel better somehow. Judas was just rotten.

Placing Judas in the greedy box is too easy, however, for we find ourselves daily in his shoes, each moment of decision a Judas moment. To act for the Good or not to act for the Good? That is the question. We act for evil often enough to know something of Judas. Those acts are definitive. They reveal our nature—fallen. We're unable to offer assistance to our friends.

But then we see Christ. Anointed, able to die to self, offering His body for His friends. We keep walking and return the moneybags, as did Judas. We recommit and die to self. It is Christ at work in us. Christ moving, through His death, to reclaim His friends.

THE BIDDING PRAYER

Help me, Lord Jesus, die to self this day. (silence)
Light of the world, shine into my darkness. (silence)
Jesus, show me how to serve the members of Your Body. (silence)
Enliven my spirit as I reveal myself to You in written word. (silence)

THE JOURNAL

Then came the day of Unleavened Bread, on which the Passover lamb had to be sacrificed. So Jesus sent Peter and John, saying, "Go and prepare the Passover meal for us that we may eat it."

Luke 22:7-8, *NRSV*

THE GOSPEL READING
Luke 22:7-14, *NRSV*

THE REFLECTION
PREPARING THE SACRIFICE

Sacrifice is coming, and Jesus knows it. It's in the air, in the culture, in the movement of the people. And the Teacher is making preparation. Luke marks the action, inviting us into its flow: water carried, a room furnished, disciples sent, food purchased and prepared. The Passover lamb will be slaughtered.

Israel is making its own preparations. They will remember the rescue God provided them from the oppression of their Egyptian slave-masters centuries earlier. An angel of death was sent at that time. Egyptians died. Israelites, who had sacrificed a lamb and used its blood on their doorjambs, were spared. Long before the Passover evening for which John and Peter are preparing, God had accomplished rescue through the slaughtering of lambs. Protection had been offered. Those who'd been looking for deliverance had been saved (see Exodus 11-12).

Christ knows the story. More important, He knows the coming sequence of God's work on this Passover. He is now the Lamb whose blood is required for Israel's rescue from their slave-master—sin. Still, those around Jesus do not understand what is happening to Him, do not understand the road He must walk. They cannot understand how God is at work on their behalf.

We're walking toward the Passion Week remembering what Christ *has* offered on our behalf. Like the disciples, we do not understand how God *is* at work on our behalf. We cannot clearly see what God is doing in the world or what Christ is in the process of bringing about. But we too have been given tasks of preparation that set the stage for God's work. We have been asked to prepare for Christ's return, to prepare for the wedding feast of the Lamb, celebrating the marriage of the Church with its groom, Christ (see Revelation 19). Christ told His disciples that He would not eat the Passover meal again "until it is fulfilled in the kingdom of God" (Luke 22:16, *RSV*). We prepare for this coming feast—for our marriage to Christ—and during Lent we remember and prepare for what we will be. "'Let us rejoice, and exult and give him the glory, for the marriage of the Lamb has come, and his Bride has made herself ready; it was granted her to be clothed with fine linen, bright and pure'—for the fine linen is the righteous deeds of the saints" (Revelation 19:7-8, *RSV*).

THE BIDDING PRAYER

Help me, Lord Jesus, die to self this day. (silence)
Light of the world, shine into my darkness. (silence)
Jesus, show me how to serve the members of Your Body. (silence)
Enliven my spirit as I reveal myself to You in written word. (silence)

THE JOURNAL

*After he had washed their feet, had put on his robe, and had returned
to the table, he said to them, "Do you know what I have done to you?
You call me Teacher and Lord—and you are right, for that is what I am.
So if I, your Lord and Teacher, have washed your feet, you also ought to
wash one another's feet. For I have set you an example, that you also
should do as I have done to you. Very truly, I tell you, servants are not
greater than their master, nor are messengers greater than the one who
sent them. If you know these things, you are blessed if you do them."*

John 13:12-17, *NRSV*

THE GOSPEL READING
John 13:1-17, *NRSV*

THE REFLECTION
LIVING THE COMMANDMENTS

John allows us a glimpse into the heart of our God. We see Jesus
waiting. Anticipating. Torture and death are coming. What does
God think about in such a circumstance? Where can His attention
lie? Imagining yourself as all-powerful, you come up with countless things to be thinking, countless things to be doing.

Christ shows us the character of God—His mettle—in an act
having nothing to do with power, nothing to do with changing

circumstances and events. Christ is concerned with love. Loving "His own" as he awaits death. It is the only action He will be about until the end—an action never given up on. We can remember His words to the lawyer concerning the greatest commandment in the Law: "'You shall love the Lord your God with all your heart, and with all your soul, and with all your mind.' This is the great and first commandment. And a second is like it, 'You shall love your neighbor as yourself.' On these two commandments depend all the law and the prophets" (Matthew 22:37-40, *NRSV*).

Christ is loving the Father—"obedient unto death, even death on a cross" (Philippians 2:8, *RSV*)—revealing this love by giving His person over to the work of God. Christ also is loving His own, caring for them through acts of service. He washes their feet, cleanses them, breaks bread and serves them.

This twofold pattern of love is to be ours during Lent and throughout our lives: loving God; loving others. Keep in mind that, like Peter, our initial reaction is to resist the humbling work of God in our lives. But also, as in Peter, the person and example of Christ will create in us the desire to surrender every part of ourselves to the work of God.

THE BIDDING PRAYER

Help me, Lord Jesus, die to self this day. (silence)
Light of the world, shine into my darkness. (silence)
Jesus, show me how to serve the members of Your Body. (silence)
Enliven my spirit as I reveal myself to You in written word. (silence)

THE JOURNAL

The angel spoke to the women: "There is nothing to fear here. I know you're looking for Jesus, the One they nailed to the cross. He is not here. He was raised, just as he said. Come and look at the place where he was placed.

"Now, get on your way quickly and tell his disciples, 'He is risen from the dead. He is going on ahead of you to Galilee. You will see him there.' That's the message."

The women, deep in wonder and full of joy lost no time in leaving the tomb. They ran to tell the disciples. Then Jesus met them, stopping them in their tracks. "Good morning!" he said. They fell to their knees, embraced his feet, and worshiped him. Jesus said, "You're holding on to me for dear life! Don't be frightened like that. Go tell my brothers that they are to go to Galilee, and that I'll meet them there."

Matthew 28:5-10, *The Message*

THE GOSPEL READING
Matthew 28:1-10, *The Message*

THE REFLECTION
REMEMBERING OUR LOVE

We've been talking about separation for a few days, thinking about how long it has been since Jesus left us. Our anticipation is up, our desire to be with Jesus heightened. We know this story of the women at the tomb, and we're itching for the second coming to be *as* real, *as* present. But alas, we're like Israel in the Sinai—no end to our wanderings in sight. We've made the move to throw off our slave-master—sin—and we're marching to the Promised Land. "But how long, O Lord? Am I to die out here in this desert without seeing You?"

On especially difficult days, my wife will sometimes turn to me, or I to her, and say, "I just wish Jesus would come back and we'd get on with heaven!" We get weary of waiting and preparing. But then we remember what Christ has accomplished, having conquered death, and through this victory given us the power to live godly lives. We revel in forgiveness. We roll around in grace. We run to the empty tomb story, read it again and run back to our lives "deep in wonder and full of joy"—remembering our Lover, keeping Him before our eyes.

So put on your favorite love song—some Sinatra maybe—and dance to this Christ, this Lover, who you can embrace and worship in wonder. Hold on to Him for dear life! And don't be frightened by this life. As He said, "Be of good cheer, I've overcome the world" (John 16:33, *RSV*).

THE BIDDING PRAYER

Risen Lord, grant me Your peace. (silence)
Christ alive, help me believe. (silence)
Jesus, show me how to feed Your sheep. (silence)
You said, "Surely I am coming soon." I say with the saints,
"Come, Lord Jesus!" (silence)

He said to them, "I have eagerly desired to eat this Passover
with you before I suffer; for I tell you, I will not eat it until
it is fulfilled in the kingdom of God."

Luke 22:15-16, *NRSV*

THE GOSPEL READING
Luke 22:15-23, *NRSV*

THE REFLECTION
A BRIGHT AND PURE BRIDE

We have already talked about the marriage feast of the Lamb, which
Christ anticipates in this conversation with the disciples. Two thousand years later, we know the marriage feast was far in humanity's
future as Jesus celebrated the Passover with His disciples. We can see
in Christ's actions an expectation of the separation as He provides
the disciples and us with an ongoing celebration. The continuing
sacrament of the Lord's Supper—communion—is something Christ
will not again share until His second coming. We are seeing in this
Scripture a dying man's last meal with His loved ones. No more
bread broken. No more wine poured out for our God.

Perhaps you've given up something for Lent; if not this year,
then in some year or years earlier. You struggle with the challenge

of abstinence, resisting the desires to taste or do something. Such Lenten observances are training, helping us remember where our desires are to be directed. A refocusing of attentions.

You have a Lover who waits in separation, who wants you to remain faithful to Him. The author of the book of Hebrews tells us that Christ sits at the right hand of God interceding for you, asking for God's gracious treatment of you (see Hebrews 7:25–8:2). There is in Jesus a focus, a tenacious concentration on His beloved Bride and her welfare.

Our task during this Lenten observance is to keep our eyes on Christ—to attend to our absent Lover and by our deeds remain pure. Judas could not do this; there was in him no capacity for waiting, no capacity to exchange desires for observance. And for such as this there is only woe. But for you there remains the celebration of the last meal, an ongoing observance and an anticipation of reunion. For such as you there is the joyful anticipation of a wedding. John tells us where all of this is leading, why waiting in purity and self-restriction is important. For when Christ returns, He will find that "'his bride has made herself ready; to her it has been granted to be clothed with fine linen, bright and pure'—for the fine linen is the righteous deeds of the saints" (Revelation 19:7-8, *NRSV*).

THE BIDDING PRAYER

Help me, Lord Jesus, die to self this day. (silence)
Light of the world, shine into my darkness. (silence)
Jesus, show me how to serve the members of Your Body. (silence)
Enliven my spirit as I reveal myself to You in written word. (silence)

THE JOURNAL

So when he had dipped the piece of bread, he gave it to Judas son of Simon Iscariot. After he received the piece of bread, Satan entered into him. Jesus said to him, "Do quickly what you are going to do." Now no one at the table knew why he said this to him.

John 13:26-28, *NRSV*

THE GOSPEL READING
John 13:18-30, *NRSV*

THE REFLECTION
THE VOID WITHIN

Judas has been concealing his thoughts—keeping a load of muck to himself—and he's ready to implode. Implosion is the right description here, for if any of us acts in ways that deny God's presence in our lives, we become hollow persons. Voids. Less and less our natural Spirit-filled selves. It's as if we're scraping out the life-giving pith at our core.

No one really wants to be hollow. So sinning usually involves that we ignore the hole we're carving in our selves. When, however, we do acknowledge a sin, we've a couple of choices before us: repentance or cover-up.

I am often struck by our boundless capacity for hiding our inner dirt. Judas has obviously honed his skills in this area to a razor's edge. Deception is now an every-moment affair for him. He's been living with these 11 disciples for a few years now. He's eaten, traveled and worked with them, even preached about Jesus with them, but none has a clue that Judas is any closer to betraying Jesus than they are themselves. Even when Jesus directly identifies Judas as the betrayer, the disciples still do not see what is missing at the heart of this man. They believe that Jesus is enlisting Judas for one more holy task when in reality Judas is heading toward the most unholy act imaginable.

Up to now, Judas has been flirting with evil, rejecting his first love. Still, Satan has not "entered him." Christ has been shielding him in some way, perhaps hoping for his repentance. Now we see what occurs when Christ withdraws from him, knowing his heart. The void is complete; the place within Judas where God used to reside is now an abyss of evil intent. A God-slayer is on the march, his woe complete.

This Lenten journey is your choice for repentance. No hiding. No ignoring your sins. You've seen Judas's road and want no part of it. You've seen your Christ and know what healing He has to offer. The choice is difficult, because it requires showing your Lover where you've pushed Him out of your heart. But you know your Lover's heart—full of patience, full of grace. As Peter tells us, the Lord "is patient with you, not wanting any to perish, but all to come to repentance" (2 Peter 3:9, *NRSV*). May we throw open these inner voids, allowing them to be refilled with the presence of our first love!

THE BIDDING PRAYER

Help me, Lord Jesus, die to self this day. (silence)
Light of the world, shine into my darkness. (silence)
Jesus, show me how to serve the members of Your Body. (silence)
Enliven my spirit as I reveal myself to You in written word. (silence)

THE JOURNAL

When he had gone out, Jesus said, "Now the Son of Man has been glorified, and God has been glorified in him."

John 13:31, *NRSV*

THE GOSPEL READING
John 13:31-35, *NRSV*

THE REFLECTION
SACRIFICE AND LOVE

40

"Son of Man" is not the first description that comes to mind when I think of Jesus. Christ's choice of this title, His careful use of it in this, His last meal with the disciples, is significant for us. He is a human being as He approaches death, and these three words place the emphasis where it must lie. Jesus is dying for humans, and He is dying *as* a human.

The Christological emphasis is important, for I've heard critics dismiss the death of Christ as meaningless, saying, "If He really was God, there's no risk in His dying. The resurrection's just a game of semantics." The Passion story will allow us none of this, however. Christ agonizes over His death because He is human and He understands just what a bleak end humanity has coming to it—separation from God, caused by our sin and finalized by death.

Death casts us off into the void where God cannot enter, where His good attributes (i.e., beauty, goodness, truth, love) do not pertain. Think of an existence devoid of goodness, love, joy, truth, beauty. Could we imagine it, we would have an image of the self encased in pure nothingness. It is what Christ contemplates as He wrestles with dying, His full divinity allowing Him to comprehend the devastation.

Nevertheless, Christ is prepared for this end—prepared for separation from the Father. The glorification has sealed Him for death and self-sacrifice in order to fulfill what is required of Him: "For the Son of Man came not to be served but to serve, and to give his life as a ransom for many" (Mark 10:45, *NRSV*). This place of "ransom"—the void of godless existence—can only be traveled by Christ. For He is the lamb without blemish—without sin—whose death opens the way of redemption for His sinful Bride, the Church. For you and me. This is what the human psyche, without sin, is capable of: self-sacrifice.

Christ knows that we're capable of this as we look *for* Him—as we look *to* Him. We're capable of sacrifice because He takes away our sinfulness, takes away the sins of the world. His sacrifice enables us, empowers us, to be like Him. That's why He confidently gives us our marching orders: "Just as I have loved you, you also should love one another" (John 13:34, *NRSV*). So let Christ pick you up this day and show everyone what you're made of. Let Him show the world that you are His disciple as you love the people around you.

THE BIDDING PRAYER

Help me, Lord Jesus, die to self this day. (silence)
Light of the world, shine into my darkness. (silence)
Jesus, show me how to serve the members of Your Body. (silence)
Enliven my spirit as I reveal myself to You in written word. (silence)

THE JOURNAL

A dispute also arose among them as to which one of
them was to be regarded as the greatest.

Luke 22:24, *NRSV*

THE GOSPEL READING

Luke 22:24-34, *NRSV*

THE REFLECTION

WEAKLING QUEENS AND KINGS

44

In Luke's Gospel, the disciples move from talking about who the traitor at the table is (see Luke 22:23) to discussing who is to be the greatest. You can imagine the conversation that must be going on. Everyone is minimizing their sins, disclaiming their capacity for treachery. Then slowly these men start detailing their faithful virtues. Pretty soon they are in a comparison contest, wondering who's to be the greatest in God's new kingdom. It's a familiar road: minimize your faults, maximize your strengths. Look good—people are watching!

I often get a look on my face, which my wife readily recognizes, even though I don't like to admit it. It's my "I'M RIGHT; THE WORLD IS WRONG!" look. Don't get in my way when I have it on. I'll eat you alive. Or if I can't do that, I'll stomp out of the room and find someplace where I can be king for a few minutes. This is a sad part of my character that I don't like to see (except when I'm expressing it, of course). I dare say, however, that it's part of all of us. We want to be kings and queens, lords and ladies, to whom everyone kowtows.

"Which of us will be the greatest?" This question doesn't sound so far from what we're capable of asking. Isn't it amazing, given this place in which we find ourselves, to read about the gift Christ offers His disciples even as they're squabbling? He gives them a kingdom. The very thing they're arguing about! Then He stands things on end, turns their world upside down. Can't they get it? Can't *we* get it? Hasn't He already washed their feet—been on His knees in front of them? It's a kingdom of servants with their Christ leading the way.

Peter's last words in this passage show us that Christ's message isn't getting through. Peter is still thinking he is on a higher plane with Christ—able to take on the world. Only Christ knows what's going on here. So, He prays for Peter not to lose his faith and to return from his coming failure with an understanding of the real task before him: giving up his self-pretension and becoming a servant.

We know Peter's story and his end. He didn't lose his faith. Church history records that he suffered the same death as Christ—a lonely crucifixion in Rome. Failure motivated him to renounce his pretensions.

As you walk through Lent remembering your weaknesses, also remember Christ's words: "My grace is enough; it's all you need. My strength comes into its own in your weakness" (2 Corinthians 12:9, *The Message*).

THE BIDDING PRAYER

Help me, Lord Jesus, die to self this day. (silence)
Light of the world, shine into my darkness. (silence)
Jesus, show me how to serve the members of Your Body. (silence)
Enliven my spirit as I reveal myself to You in written word. (silence)

THE JOURNAL

"If you know me, you will know my Father also. From now on you do know him and have seen him." Philip said to him, "Lord, show us the Father, and we will be satisfied." Jesus said to him, "Have I been with you all this time, Philip, and you still do not know me?"

John 14:7-9, *NRSV*

THE GOSPEL READING
John 14:1-14, *NRSV*

48

THE REFLECTION
SILENCE IN US ALL VOICES BUT YOUR OWN

My family has a weekly rhythm of hiking on our day off. Before starting this Sabbath hike, we read a psalm and recite this prayer: "Lord, silence in us all voices but Your own. That in hearing, we may believe. And in believing, we may obey. To the glory of Your name." Hear; believe; obey. It's a trifold pattern found throughout Scripture. It's not a pattern we take to easily, nor does modernity help us adopt it. Most of our days are full of things that block our God-hearing: radio and television programs, phone conversations, Internet teasers, and the chattering of our own desires. Belief is not a state of mind prized in our culture. Knowledge, competence and action are the stuff of winners. What of obedience? If it's to something other than our self-direction, we rugged individualists want none of it.

Don't beat yourself up too much, however, for in this passage we see the disciples having their own troubles with the pattern. They're stuck somewhere between the first two folds, somewhere between hearing and believing—not yet having heard, not yet believing what they have been told. They're looking for something tangible—visible, empirical. They're seeking an earthly mansion, a brick-'n'-mortar kingdom; they want to see the Father, as they would see a camel or a donkey.

Why do we have such a hard time experiencing the Kingdom, seeing the Father and believing Jesus? Some of us have little training in seeing the things of God. But even those who've had training, like the disciples, find it challenging to unclench from the empirical.

But then eternity breaks through, catching us unawares. We imagine things that last, that neither moth nor rust can corrupt. We think outside the present, anticipating and remembering, free-ranging over time. We contemplate abstractions—like numbers and concepts, like beauty and perfection. We see a part of ourselves that won't be chained down, even in a society where we're instructed to believe in pretty faces and full bank accounts.

We know there's more in this life than is dreamed of in *O* magazine and "reality" TV. The crumbling, decaying empirical world tunes our desires into eternity. We look at what God is doing: rescuing lives, changing sinners' hearts, granting peace to the dying. These glimmers of Kingdom life help to silence the clamor of voices so that we can hear, believe and obey.

THE BIDDING PRAYER

Help me, Lord Jesus, die to self this day. (silence)
Light of the world, shine into my darkness. (silence)
Jesus, show me how to serve the members of Your Body. (silence)
Enliven my spirit as I reveal myself to You in written word. (silence)

THE JOURNAL

*"I will not leave you orphaned; I am coming to you.
In a little while the world will no longer see me,
but you will see me; because I live, you also will live."*
John 14:18-19, *NRSV*

THE GOSPEL READING
John 14:15-31, *NRSV*

THE REFLECTION
AGAINST LONELINESS

This evening as I write, my friend is dying in a hospital hundreds of miles away. He's 95 and has lived a long, rich life. I've depended on his intercessory prayer for a number of years—he's been like a holy antivirus program running in the background while I've been going about my daily living. I'm glad the sufferings of his life will be eased, but I'm saddened that the world will lose such a humble servant. I want him to be with God, but I don't want to be left without his presence in the world. The loneliness is already creeping in.

Jesus knows how our hearts work. He's lived as a human being and understands this kind of loneliness. He knows the feelings that will flood through the disciples as they lose their teacher—the fear that will soon overtake them—this fear that will eat at them, telling them, "You're alone. Nothing but death, sorrow and darkness for you!" These are the voices of the "ruler of this world" who is also coming for them.

You know these voices. You hear them each day when the news is churning. You feel them whispering as friends die, as lovers are hooked to feeding tubes, as children break their arms, as you wait for test results from the doctor. You begin to believe with the poet Rilke that "we are unutterably alone, essentially, especially in the things most intimate and most important to us."[1] This is how our heart works when it's left alone.

What help can this Christ hope to offer us? It is singularly significant (essential, in fact) that He offers nothing by Himself, nothing alone. Only through His obedience to the Father—living in relationship with God—does He become an advocate and intercessor able to do us any good. And in requesting that another be sent to be present with us during His absence, He is both acknowledging submission to God's sacrificial work and acknowledging the deep importance of our relationship to Him.

He shows in His living how love and commandment-keeping (love and obedience) are bound together. Such a one as this is able to offer us help—freedom from orphaning, freedom from fear, true peace. This obedient living, this submission to God's will, is where the Spirit of truth is leading us.

Rise. Be on your way this day. And if you love this Christ in return, keep His words! For you are unutterably loved.

THE BIDDING PRAYER

Help me, Lord Jesus, die to self this day. (silence)
Light of the world, shine into my darkness. (silence)
Jesus, show me how to serve the members of Your Body. (silence)
Enliven my spirit as I reveal myself to You in written word. (silence)

THE JOURNAL

55

*Then [Jesus] said to them, "So thick-headed! So slow-hearted!
Why can't you simply believe all that the prophets said? Don't you see
that these things had to happen, that the Messiah had to suffer and only
then enter into his glory?" Then he started at the beginning, with the
Books of Moses, and went on through all the Prophets, pointing out
everything in the Scriptures that referred to him.*

*They came to the edge of the village where they were headed. He acted
as if he were going on but they pressed him: "Stay and have supper with
us. It's nearly evening; the day is done." So he went in with them.
And here is what happened: He sat down at the table with them. Taking
the bread, he blessed and broke and gave it to them. At that moment,
open-eyed, wide-eyed, they recognized him. And then he disappeared.*

Luke 24:25-31, *The Message*

THE GOSPEL READING
Luke 24:13-31, *The Message*

THE REFLECTION
CHRIST-OPENED EYES

"Blockhead!" "Slow-heart!" Not exactly terms you'd like your God to be using to describe you. I can hear my five-year-old son correcting Jesus now, "That's definitely *not* a nice thing to say. We don't call people names!" Jesus' response: "Yeah, Yeah, I *know*. But these guys really *are* thick-heads."

"Braveheart!" "Razormind!" Now, *that's* more like it. Here are names we'd imagine ourselves being called by Jesus. Funny though, even a couple of thousand years after the Resurrection, with centuries of God's work in the Church, how easy it is to stop believing the work of God in Christ. We find ourselves completely confused about what God is doing in the world. Then someone steps in and helps us to see what's in Scripture. The Spirit reveals the work of God to us in our studies and prayer. We recognize Jesus. Our eyes are opened . . . wide.

It should be some comfort to us that Jesus takes such interest in moving us along in our understanding of His ways. He wants us to "get it," to get in on what He's doing. This takes some patience and even—sometimes—a little healthy *calling it like it is*. Rejoice this day that we're not relegated to blockhead status. Christ will keep teaching while we keep struggling to open our eyes to Him.

THE BIDDING PRAYER

Risen Lord, grant me Your peace. (silence)
Christ alive, help me believe. (silence)
Jesus, show me how to feed Your sheep. (silence)
You said, "Surely I am coming soon." I say with the saints,
"Come, Lord Jesus!" (silence)

PART TWO

THE SECOND 10 DAYS

"I am the vine, you are the branches. Those who abide in me and I in them bear much fruit, because apart from me you can do nothing."

John 15:5, *NRSV*

THE GOSPEL READING
John 15:1-11, *NRSV*

THE REFLECTION
CHRIST-FIREWORKS

60

I've grown blueberries in my backyard for a number of years, and I have one bush that has done exceptionally well since its first season as a starter plant. It was the first bush to bear fruit of the six with which I began. Some years the produce from it has been more than the other five plants combined. I like the plant so much that I've tried my hand at rooting plants from its cut branches, sadly with little luck. Watching this plant has helped me understand God's desire to see us bearing fruit. Our lives, when they bear the characteristics of God's person (love, joy, patience, kindness, generosity, faithfulness, gentleness, self-control [see Galatians 5:22-23]), are pleasing to God.

Metaphors such as the vine and branch lead us to connect our everyday living with the kingdom of heaven and help us see Jesus in the quotidian. Where do you see fruit being born in your life? In children or students? In stock funds, jobs or prayers? Such harvests give you some idea of what it feels like to be a farmer with a bumper crop—some small idea of what God hopes for you. "Easy pickin's!"

Last summer, I went with my family to a commercial blueberry farm a few miles up the road. The bushes there dwarfed my plants, looking like row upon row of green and blue fireworks. The berries hung heavy in clusters—large, bulbous, and a deeply ripe cobalt blue. Here was picking I'd only dreamed of at home, picking that made you tired, picking requiring that you move from one bush to another just so you didn't get bored. My kids were in heaven, sitting under bushes, munching in the shade of the arching branches, moving from bush to bush, tasting, chomping. I wanted my bushes to grow into this abundance! I asked for tips from the farmer and went home hoping to help all my plants along, not just my best one, for they all had a long way to go.

God is working the same way for us, desiring to produce bursting, bulbous, ripe Christ-fireworks. Some of us have more and larger berries. Some of us have more fungus (i.e., sin) clinging to our branches. Some of us need to be pruned. But we've all got a Gardener who knows what a good bush looks like and how to get His garden in shape. Our Gardener loves getting little plants into production, loves seeing the harvest, and won't leave us untended.

For your part, little plants of God? Stick to the branch. Stick to Christ. Explode at your tips with a harvest full of Him.

THE BIDDING PRAYER

Help me, Lord Jesus, die to self this day. (silence)
Light of the world, shine into my darkness. (silence)
Jesus, show me how to serve the members of Your Body. (silence)
Enliven my spirit as I reveal myself to You in written word. (silence)

THE JOURNAL

"And I appointed you to go and bear fruit, fruit that will last, so that the Father will give you whatever you ask him in my name. I am giving you these commands so that you may love one another."

John 15:16-17, *NRSV*

THE GOSPEL READING
John 15:12-17, *NRSV*

THE REFLECTION
KINGDOM-SEEKING LIVING

64

Brown bananas. Bruised peaches. Rotten grapes. We know all about fruit that doesn't last. The produce man tries to hide it from us. We use refrigeration and canning to ward off decay, but at times all our efforts appear fruit*less*. With the psalmist, we exasperate, "We don't last long. Like our dogs, we age and weaken. And die" (Psalm 49:12, *The Message*).

Christ knows all about this. He's walking toward death, toward becoming a rotting corpse. Torturers are prowling for Him while He attempts to get His message through to the disciples. Death all around, and Christ is talking about commandments, fruit and love. How perplexing this conversation seems!

Then we remember how perplexing ordinary day-to-day existence is with objects decaying all around us: cracked plaster, carpet stains, broken skin. We need to eat every six hours because surfeit lasts only so long. A bottomless void resides in us that nothing seems to fill. No, Christ's conversation isn't perplexing when we think about it. The *void*, that's what smacks of bewilderment, hits us square in the face as being perplexing. A mission with commands, a love-quest, lasting fruit: These things sound real, sound expansively filling. In this light, "reality" and "Christ's kingdom" strike us as synonyms.

In C. S. Lewis's *The Silver Chair,* the character Puddleglum is resisting the efforts of an enchantress holding him and three companions hostage in an underground kingdom. She's trying to bewitch them into thinking they've never seen the sun or their homeland above ground, or Aslan (the Jesus-figure in the story). Puddleglum shakes himself free of the enchantment and says:

Suppose we *have* only dreamed, or made up, all those things—trees and grass and sun and stars and Aslan himself. Suppose we have. Then all I can say is that, in that case, the made-up things seem a good deal more important than the real ones. Suppose this black pit of a kingdom of yours *is* the only world. Well, it strikes me as a pretty poor one. And that's a funny thing, when you come to think of it. We're just babies making up a game, if you're right. But four babies playing a game can make a play-world which licks your real world hollow. That's why I'm going to stand by the play world. I'm on Aslan's side even if there isn't any Aslan to lead it. I'm going to live as like a Narnian as I can even if there isn't any Narnia.[2]

We've set forth this Lent to spend our lives looking for God's kingdom. We're living as much like a Christian as we can. Loving without regard for self. Becoming fruit to be eaten by our neighbors. We're accomplishing this as friends of Christ, knowing what He knows. This isn't the American dream—and that's a good thing. It's the kingdom of God—the inverted priorities of Jesus.

THE BIDDING PRAYER

Help me, Lord Jesus, die to self this day. (silence)
Light of the world, shine into my darkness. (silence)
Jesus, show me how to serve the members of Your Body. (silence)
Enliven my spirit as I reveal myself to You in written word. (silence)

THE JOURNAL

_____
_____
_____
_____
_____
_____
_____
_____

*"If the world hates you, be aware that it hated me before it hated you.
If you belonged to the world, the world would love you as its own.
Because you do not belong to the world, but I have chosen you out
of the world—therefore the world hates you."*

John 15:18-19, *NRSV*

THE GOSPEL READING
John 15:18-27, *NRSV*

THE REFLECTION
BEING HATED

Jesus' conversation turns without pause from a love-command to a hate-warning. We've readied ourselves for one action and now we're directed to think about its opposite. Warning signs fly up. Oxygen masks drop. "TURBULENCE AHEAD!" It's as if Christ is giving us His version of Newton's law: For every action there is an equal and opposite reaction. Now we can't help pondering who's against us.

If you're like me, you have difficulty bringing to mind people who really hate you—that bone-crunching kind of hate you find in the psalms. The best I can manage are some recollections of being introduced to people at parties when I was a minister years ago. I'd be enjoying a conversation, listening to casual expletives, and then it would happen. Somebody would tell the guy with the colorful talk that I was a pastor. Instantly the conversation turned angelic, and often the "offending party" would not continue speaking until I was out of earshot. I had become too "holy." My occupation had produced an opposing reaction. Not a very challenging situation, but it's the only hated-for-my-faith story I have.

Polite contempt is perhaps the worst mistreatment Western Christians face. Nonetheless, there are beings in this world that hate us and seek our overthrow. Their contempt for things holy is real; but unlike our colorfully tongued neighbors, these beings will not walk away, leaving us to our God. These forces of evil (whatever you care to title them) hate our souls and are desirous of eradicating our love-acts.

We see their hatred most acutely when we're tempted. How many times in the past two weeks have circumstances been ripe to make you drop your Lenten disciplines—the cookies on the counter when you've given them up, the tantalizing pictures of what you're not supposed to be about. Tormentors are stalking us just as they did Christ in the wilderness (see Mark 1:12-13); we *do* have something that hates us with a passion!

Luckily, the laws of spiritual action and reaction are not balanced like Newton's laws of motion. There is no reaction that can destroy Christ's love-work in us. Walk about today and, as Christ commands, testify to this: "In all these things we are more than conquerors through him who loved us. For I am sure that neither death, nor life, nor angels, nor principalities, nor things present, nor things to come, nor powers, nor height, nor depth, nor anything else in all creation, will be able to separate us from the love of God in Christ Jesus our Lord" (Romans 8:37-39, *RSV*).

THE BIDDING PRAYER

Help me, Lord Jesus, die to self this day. (silence)
Light of the world, shine into my darkness. (silence)
Jesus, show me how to serve the members of Your Body. (silence)
Enliven my spirit as I reveal myself to You in written word. (silence)

THE JOURNAL

_____

_____

_____

_____

_____

_____

_____

_____

_____

_____

_____

"Nevertheless I tell you the truth: it is to your advantage that I go away, for if I do not go away, the Advocate will not come to you; but if I go, I will send him to you. And when he comes, he will prove the world wrong about sin and righteousness and judgment . . ."

John 16:7-8, *NRSV*

THE GOSPEL READING
John 16:1-11, *NRSV*

THE REFLECTION
LIVING IN A WAR ZONE

We joined a war when we joined the Church—we picked a side. And though the book of Revelation assures us that we've joined the winning side, our existential position is precarious. It's as if we've signed up for the French Resistance months before D-day. Overwhelming help is coming, the battle will swing our way, but we're likely to be killed or entrapped before the victory. One has to believe in the rightness of one's choice under such circumstances, the justness of one's side. One needs to be steeled for hard times ahead. Christ is putting steel in our bones through His departing words. He wants us on our feet, unfettered and ready for the difficulties of living as disciples—for living in a war zone.

In light of this, it's funny how passively and calmly the Church is viewed by many outsiders when all along it's more like covert ops. Calling the Church passive is simply to misunderstand the weapons of its resistance. An examination of the armor imagery in Ephesians shows how crazy we must appear. We're given a belt (i.e., truth), a flak jacket (i.e., righteousness), war boots (i.e., the gospel of peace), a shield (i.e., faith), a helmet (i.e., salvation), and a sword (i.e., the Word of God) (see Ephesians 6:13-17). If our armor doesn't strike you as just the least bit strange, then you've been in the Church a long time. From our enemy's perspective, it's as if we're strapping bull's-eyes on our backs. "Just what kind of war do you think you're going to?" I can hear them taunt.

Luckily for us, the Spirit of God was sent to prove what constitutes true victory. Because of Christ's sacrifice, we're able to have the living God residing in us—something never possible before Jesus' death and resurrection. Christ's departure means that we have God, not next to us in the person of Christ, but within us in the person of the Spirit. The Spirit proves that the remedy for sin, the gift of righteousness, and the control of judgment flow from above, where Christ is seated next to God. Victory is assured through sacrifice, servitude and obedience—strange weapons indeed!

The assurance provided by the Spirit allows us to see our sacrifices in a new light. We can turn the worldly Epicurean slogan—"Eat, drink, and be merry, for tomorrow we die!"—on its head: "Fast, pray, and love, for tomorrow we die, and the day after tomorrow resurrection in Christ!"

The Bidding Prayer

Help me, Lord Jesus, die to self this day. (silence)
Light of the world, shine into my darkness. (silence)
Jesus, show me how to serve the members of Your Body. (silence)
Enliven my spirit as I reveal myself to You in written word. (silence)

The Journal

"When the Spirit of truth comes, he will guide you into all the truth; for he will not speak on his own, but will speak whatever he hears, and he will declare to you the things that are to come. He will glorify me, because he will take what is mine and declare it to you. All that the Father has is mine. For this reason I said that he will take what is mine and declare it to you."

John 16:13-15, *NRSV*

THE GOSPEL READING
John 16:12-15, *NRSV*

THE REFLECTION
JESUS PIPES

My wife tells the story of a class she took with Dale Bruner at Whitworth College in which he described the work of the Holy Spirit. Dr. Bruner would stand behind the blackboard, reach his hand around the side with his index finger extended and point to the word "Jesus" written there. "That's the work of the Holy Spirit," he would tell the class. "To point to Jesus."

The Spirit confirms that it is one with the Father and Son through the character of its work: self-sacrifice. This third person of the Godhead gives glory to another. Finger extended, it directs us to

Jesus. We have a holy road-sign, or holy positioning system, built right into us in order to triangulate and pinpoint the Word made flesh. God-speak and truth, living-word and veracity are merged in this Being and so joined to us.

I'm traveling in a car down a mountain pass as I write, looking out on my right at a cascading stream—roiling waters drawn toward the Chesapeake. The movement of the bubbles and up-flows are usually captivating, but today I find myself thinking about the streambed that carries the water. It's a symbol for the Spirit—a channel for the water of life flowing from the Lamb (see Revelation 22), always solid, never raising itself up. A holy cascade-conduit.

All that the Father has flows to Jesus; all that Jesus has flows to the Holy Spirit; all that the Spirit has flows to us. Waterfalls of blessing—word, empowerment and truth cascaded through us to one another. Nothing held back. All given away—sacrificially.

There is joy in this work—being a conduit for Christ's beauty, truth and goodness—difficult though it is. The water of life is heavy with the weight of *Being*, all those attributes of God. They are dense and more real than all that is fading around us. The "weight of glory" is an accurate description. The heaviness of holiness can seem too much to bear, the word of Christ too much to stand. Yet we have a companion, a signpost given by Christ, whose presence enables us to bear this wonderful thing—the Word of God.

Emulate the Spirit this day, piping Jesus into the deserts of the world. Refresh the dying ones around you. While you're at it, strap on one of those oversized sports fan's gloves and point it toward Jesus!

THE BIDDING PRAYER

Help me, Lord Jesus, die to self this day. (silence)
Light of the world, shine into my darkness. (silence)
Jesus, show me how to serve the members of Your Body. (silence)
Enliven my spirit as I reveal myself to You in written word. (silence)

THE JOURNAL

"Are you discussing among yourselves what I meant when I said, 'A little while, and you will no longer see me, and again a little while, and you will see me'? Very truly, I tell you, you will weep and mourn, but the world will rejoice; you will have pain, but your pain will turn into joy. When a woman is in labor, she has pain, because her hour has come. But when her child is born, she no longer remembers the anguish because of the joy of having brought a human being into the world. So you have pain now; but I will see you again, and your hearts will rejoice, and no one will take your joy from you."

John 16:19-22, *NRSV*

THE GOSPEL READING
John 16:16-24, *NRSV*

THE REFLECTION
A JOY THAT CANNOT BE STOLEN

Today I've been told about an unborn baby's death—eight months in the mother, but not yet in the world. Unanticipated death delivered to expectant parents. The news is devastating and present. My children have asked question after question over lunch, trying to get an understanding of why it happened, how it happened, why nothing could be done to fix it. They've recalled their own birth stories and wondered about all the things that might have happened to them. The continued conversation became so difficult that I pulled out one of my weapons of last resort: "This is the *last* question about this; now, go ahead . . ."

This is the kind of pain that will smother the disciples within 24 hours. They don't understand what's coming, nor are they clued in to this conversation. Jesus' death will be for them unexpected. Tragic. Final. Christ is telling them about it before it happens, telling them their pain will not be the end of His story, will not be the end of the gospel. Still, they're not hearing Him. They're ready for Jesus' birth as Messiah, pregnant with His world mission. They're thinking, *Surely He'll burst on the world-power stage soon and set things right.* Judas knows that Jesus won't do *this*, though he doesn't comprehend what he *will* do. A belly full of pain for these disciples by next evening! What's on the verge of exploding to life, to power, will be dead. Christ is trying to help them apprehend this as the darkness descends.

In our present state, it's an important fact that we've a Savior who looks to our future—preparing us for it, preparing us a place in it, preparing to make our joy complete. We continue living with darkness all around and find ourselves daily wanting Christ's return. We want this resurrection future where deep pains are healed—where unborn children have no hindrances to life and growth. So we keep looking for this Christ and hang on His words, "I will see you again, and your hearts will rejoice, and no one will take your joy from you."

THE BIDDING PRAYER

Help me, Lord Jesus, die to self this day. (silence)
Light of the world, shine into my darkness. (silence)
Jesus, show me how to serve the members of Your Body. (silence)
Enliven my spirit as I reveal myself to You in written word. (silence)

THE JOURNAL

While they were saying all this, Jesus appeared to them and said,
"Peace be with you." They thought they were seeing a ghost and were
scared half to death. He continued with them, "Don't be upset, and don't
let all these doubting questions take over. Look at my hands; look at my
feet—it's really me. Touch me. Look me over from head to toe. A ghost
doesn't have muscle and bone like this." As he said this, he showed them
his hands and feet. They still couldn't believe what they were seeing.
It was too much; it seemed too good to be true.

He asked, "Do you have any food here?" They gave him a piece of
leftover fish they had cooked. He took it and ate it right before their eyes.

Luke 24:32-43, *The Message*

THE GOSPEL READING
Luke 24:32-43, *The Message*

THE REFLECTION
REAL PEACE-GIVING

"The Passing of the Peace" is a practice my church shares from time
to time. The minister instructs us to stand, turn to our neighbors
and share the peace of Christ with them. We usually shake hands
and offer a greeting. Some people say, "The peace of Christ be with
you," while others smile awkwardly and say, "Hi!" The practice is

meant to remind us of Christ's peace-granting work in the world and to invite us to become participants in His peace-work by sharing it with others. I've never had the chance to offer the peace to anyone who really looked frightened. The whole affair is usually quite casual, often transitioning into a chat-time about events of the week past or coming. Only once in a while do you come face to face with someone actually thinking about the significance of the act rather than feeling awkward about what they're going to say.

Today's Scripture makes these church experiences of passing the peace seem too genteel. Perhaps we ought to give each other a good fright before sharing the peace—lay a good scare on our sisters and brothers in Christ. We've material enough in our lives to produce these. Like the disciples, we're full of doubting questions from day to day, beset with problems, sicknesses and deaths. We attend church with polite Christian faces, glossing over our and others' problems—never letting them be real enough to need a true peace-passing.

Next time you're somewhere when the peace of Christ is being passed, remember what you're frightened of. Give yourself a good scare and see Jesus, flesh 'n' bones, in the face of the person right before you.

THE BIDDING PRAYER

Risen Lord, grant me Your peace. (silence)
Christ alive, help me believe. (silence)
Jesus, show me how to feed Your sheep. (silence)
You said, "Surely I am coming soon." I say with the saints,
"Come, Lord Jesus!" (silence)

His disciples said, "Yes, now you are speaking plainly, not in any figure of speech! Now we know that you know all things, and do not need to have anyone question you; by this we believe that you came from God." Jesus answered them, "Do you now believe? The hour is coming, indeed it has come, when you will be scattered, each one to his home, and you will leave me alone. Yet I am not alone because the Father is with me. I have said this to you, so that in me you may have peace. In the world you face persecution. But take courage; I have conquered the world!"

John 16:29-33, *NRSV*

THE GOSPEL READING
John 16:25-33, *NRSV*

THE REFLECTION
THE GOSPEL TRUTH

Plain talk, straight up, the gospel truth—the kind of talk we'd like from the people around us. The talk we dream about from our politicians (emphasis on "dream"). It's speech we only get from people with nothing to lose, people not out to *get* something from someone. But the funny thing is, it's also the kind of talk we can't often handle; it gets in the way of what we want to do in the world, and we *don't* want reality interfering with our projects.

Christ has been talking with these disciples in figures of speech the past few years; parables and stories have been His mainstay. He knows them and their capacities. He's been wooing these 11 disciples and all humanity like a lover who knows what his partner can handle. There's been a real need to get human beings away from their preoccupations and on to the things of God's kingdom. Christ's object: to have us believe in Him, believe that He and the Father are one, believe that He's the Messiah, the only salvation. The wooing has worked! These men and many others have fallen in love with this man, believing in His God-ordained mission. They've left their nets, given up their projects in return for His love. Well, almost.

There's still an element of misbelief that hasn't been eliminated. See how they want to rest their belief on omniscience—*as if that's something Christ would emphasize*! Here we have God living out sacrifice and servanthood, dying in obedience for love of the Father and humanity. Even at this late hour, the disciples are confused about this, about the Father's work in Jesus.

They'll be scattered in a few hours. As Jesus says, "You're about to make a run for it—saving your own skins and abandoning me" (John 16:32, *The Message*). They'll be unable to do what they want, i.e., save Jesus' skin. And as their trust in themselves is destroyed, Christ's obedient death will provide a rescue for all of us. It's the upside-down nature of our salvation—through no strength of our own, but only through Christ. It's the plain talk we all need—straight talk from Jesus: "You're going to fall flat on your faces. But take courage; I've conquered the world!"

THE BIDDING PRAYER

Help me, Lord Jesus, die to self this day. (silence)
Light of the world, shine into my darkness. (silence)
Jesus, show me how to serve the members of Your Body. (silence)
Enliven my spirit as I reveal myself to You in written word. (silence)

THE JOURNAL

*After Jesus had spoken these words, he looked up to heaven
and said, "Father, the hour has come; glorify your Son so that
the Son may glorify you . . ."*

John 17:1, *NRSV*

THE GOSPEL READING
John 17:1-5, *NRSV*

THE REFLECTION
THE COMING STORM

There's a storm brewing, a late winter nor'easter hugging the
Eastern coast of the United States. My town has been in preparation mode for hours as the storm makes its approach. It seems in
no hurry to unleash its banks of snow. I've tracked it on the com-
puter radar, trying to determine its estimated time of arrival; and
having made the trip for snowblower gas, milk and Disney videos,
I'm ready—waiting for the moment when duty calls me to the side-
walks and driveway. It's silly, all this frenzy the weatherman stirs
me to. But then, one doesn't want to be caught unprepared!

Jesus has been following a storm of His own. It's been churning for eons, engulfing everything in its path. Lives have been
lost. Continents ripped up and destroyed. "The whole creation has
been groaning in travail" (Romans 8:22, *RSV*) under its onslaught.

Christ has been preparing to dig us out of our sin-storm—He's been getting ready to make a rescue. When the storm broke, He was in the presence of the Father, giving glory and receiving glory. Later, He flew into our hurricane, spending 30 years watching it rage around Him, spending another three years probing its walls. Finishing the work that God gave Him to do.

Now the time has arrived to silence this storm. Christ knows what it will take to push the sin-drifts and hate-piles out of our lives, out of the world. He's had some practice calming the stormy travails in nature, hushing the sea storms. Now He's becoming a high-pressure dome to push the guilt clouds away, to usher sunshine and warmth back into sin-darkened lives. Our driveways will be cleared, our life-ways unclogged.

Our Lenten journey through the Gospels is a close-up look at humanity's storm map. We're seeing the last wild blasts of sin's power. The hour has come—the fullness of time. Christ is prepared, and nothing can withstand His grace-front—His death recasting our spiritual weather scene.

But when the fullness of time had come, God sent his Son, born of a woman, born under the law, in order to redeem those who were under the law, so that we might receive adoption as children. And because you are children, God has sent the Spirit of his Son into our hearts, crying "Abba! Father!" So you are no longer a slave but a child, and if a child then an heir, through God (Galatians 4:4-7, *NRSV*).

THE BIDDING PRAYER

Help me, Lord Jesus, die to self this day. (silence)
Light of the world, shine into my darkness. (silence)
Jesus, show me how to serve the members of Your Body. (silence)
Enliven my spirit as I reveal myself to You in written word. (silence)

THE JOURNAL

"But now I am coming to you, and I speak these things in the world so that they may have my joy made complete in themselves. I have given them your word, and the world has hated them because they do not belong to the world, just as I do not belong to the world. I am not asking you to take them out of the world, but I ask you to protect them from the evil one. They do not belong to the world, just as I do not belong to the world. Sanctify them in the truth . . ."

John 17:13-17, *NRSV*

94

THE GOSPEL READING
John 17:6-26, *NRSV*

THE REFLECTION
SLEEPING TIGHT

Each night after laying my three-year-old daughter in her bed, I proceed to pray for her. I have a standard prayer, which remains largely the same from night to night and has five or six stanzas. One of the stanzas is: "And keep the evil one far, far from her!" After my daughter learned there were bad people in the world, she started stopping me after this part and adding, "*And* the bad guys, Daddy!" From time to time she asks me who this "evil one" is and why he doesn't like her. With much practice, I think bedtime theology lessons are getting easier for me. Some nights I wish I had someone to explain theodicy to me before closing my eyes.

Jesus cares for us even more dearly than the best parents are able, more dearly than siblings, friends or lovers. And these verses show that He knows what provides security. It's bedtime for the world; time for Him to tuck us in, close the door with the nightlight on and get to work. The big brother charged by the Father with looking after His siblings; or to use a different image, the lover putting to bed his sweetheart before leaving to work through the night on her behalf. Both images capture this scene in John. Here is one who loves those being left and wants nothing to happen to them while He's gone. What is this Christ doing to secure them, to secure us? He's praying to the Father. Prayers offered on the disciples' behalf, prayers offered for those who will find Jesus through their words, i.e., you and me. He's tucking us in tightly and commending us to the Father, who is the source of security.

Christ knows the truth of Luther's verse: "Tho' this world with devils filled should threaten to undo us . . ." but He also knows the love of the Father can keep us through all evil. Christ our big brother, Christ our bridegroom, has made Himself holy and pure (sanctified) that we too might rest in the presence of God, one with each other, one with Christ and one with God. As with my daughter, I can leave you, too, with these words, "Sleep tight, little one!"

THE BIDDING PRAYER

Help me, Lord Jesus, die to self this day. (silence)
Light of the world, shine into my darkness. (silence)
Jesus, show me how to serve the members of Your Body. (silence)
Enliven my spirit as I reveal myself to You in written word. (silence)

THE JOURNAL

He came out and went, as was his custom, to the Mount of Olives; and the disciples followed him. When he reached the place, he said to them, "Pray that you may not come into the time of trial." Then he withdrew from them about a stone's throw, knelt down, and prayed . . .

Luke 22:39-41, *NRSV*

THE GOSPEL READING
Luke 22:39-46, *NRSV*

THE REFLECTION
WAKING UP TO JESUS

Where do you turn when you're stressed? What comes to the fore? If you're like me, you're a mixed bag of habits—some good, some bad. Prayer, overeating, exercise, overdrinking, journaling, over-sleeping, meditation, sex, psalmody, movies—we mix and match the healthy and the diseased when we're stressed. We're unsteady creatures—who of us could point the finger at these disciples for not staying awake to pray? Next to Jesus, we look like spiritual vagrants. *He* is another matter altogether.

Luke catches Jesus in one of His habits—gives us a reality show's behind-the-scenes look at Him. The long Last Supper discourse in John's Gospel, which has occupied our attention for days now, showed us a man constantly in prayer. Luke provides a new take on this habit, showing Jesus walking into the night to a place "as was his custom." It's a habit visible enough to have caught the eye of witnesses who would tell Luke about it years later when he was writing his Gospel. Jesus, walking to a consecrated place, to His prayer knoll—a scene of which many were aware. How often has He done this in His lifetime? Did He form the habit on His first trip to Jerusalem when He was *12*? That trip where His parents lost Him, only to find Him the next day sitting in the temple, teaching the "holy men"? That trip where He said, "Why were you searching for me? Did you not know that I must be in my Father's house" (Luke 2:49, *NRSV*)? Finding a holy spot to be with His Father is not *second* nature to this man; it's first nature—instinctual, innate.

And here we are, in the sleeping bag with the drowsy disciples. Needing coffee—strong coffee! Walking through Lent, unable to keep ourselves on task for even "one hour." It helps to realize that even Jesus needs help. As Joel Green highlights in his commentary on this passage, angels come to help Jesus when it gets hard—just as they ministered to Him in the wilderness (see Matthew 4:11).[3] And Christ's admonition—"Get up! Pray so you won't give in to temptation" (Luke 22:46, *The Message*)—points back to expertise gained through withstanding temptations in the wilderness. Prayer and divine aid sent because of prayer got Him through.

If you find yourself wobbling your way through Lent—a spiritual sleepyhead—listen to the gentle words of your Savior calling with blood and sweat on His brow: "Hey, wake up. Get busy praying. You can stand up to these temptations. I'm at your side with the strength you need!"

THE BIDDING PRAYER

Help me, Lord Jesus, die to self this day. (silence)
Light of the world, shine into my darkness. (silence)
Jesus, show me how to serve the members of Your Body. (silence)
Enliven my spirit as I reveal myself to You in written word. (silence)

THE JOURNAL

_____

_____

_____

_____

_____

_____

_____

_____

_____

_____

PART THREE

THE THIRD
10 DAYS

And going a little farther, he threw himself on the ground and prayed that, if it were possible, the hour might pass from him. He said, "Abba, Father, for you all things are possible; remove this cup from me; yet, not what I want, but what you want." He came and found them sleeping; and he said to Peter, "Simon, are you asleep? Could you not keep awake one hour?"

Mark 14:35-37, *NRSV*

THE GOSPEL READING
Mark 14:32-42, *NRSV*

104

THE REFLECTION
THE THIRD SHIFT

I'm in charge of the nighttime routines in our house, the shadow jobs of the third shift. My wife is the early bird in the family, which grants her privileged status on breakfast detail. Breakfast is first shift work—I can't recall the last time I was awake for the start of first shift (though my wife probably does).

The most important activity on third shift is midnight potty detail. At this stage in our children's lives, they sleep about 11 hours, but their bodies aren't prepared to make it more than 8 without a potty break. So I gently pick them up from their beds at midnight, get them to the potty and try to stir them enough to complete their mission. It's a tough task given they've been asleep for 4 hours. I think sometimes they get through the entire routine without rousing. I gave up trying to get them cognitively engaged a few months ago—too many tears with that approach. No, one can do *just fine* going potty while asleep, *if* one has a good spotter.

Praying is not a task that's usually high on my third-shift list. It's not a task that my children would let me assign them during those hours. Prayer is strenuous work, requiring concentration. It can make you drowsy and tired at the best of times. Here we find the disciples on third shift, being assigned prayer detail. And here we find them failing three times.

Yet we see Jesus, hard at work, praying, flung upon the ground— His body an instrument of petition contrasting sharply against the resting, sleeping, heavy-eyed bodies of His disciples. He's grieving, distressed, agitated to the point of dying—still He continues to pray. Not heavy-handed prayer, but firm, respectful petition that submits itself to the will of the Father. The Gospel writers are leaving us no room for misunderstanding. *We* are not able to play a role in our salvation. The battle is too intense for humanity; we are too drained of life and alertness.

We cannot survive without this Christ who works through the night as we sleep, who accepts the work given Him by the father— who accepts His cup. This Christ becomes the one upon whom all humanity's waste is dumped—all the muck, abuse and sin of our lives—while we, too groggy to wake, keep sleeping.

THE BIDDING PRAYER

Help me, Lord Jesus, die to self this day. (silence)
Light of the world, shine into my darkness. (silence)
Jesus, show me how to serve the members of Your body. (silence)
Enliven my spirit as I reveal myself to You in written word. (silence)

THE JOURNAL

*While he was still speaking, suddenly a crowd came, and the
one called Judas, one of the twelve, was leading them. He approached
Jesus to kiss him; but Jesus said to him . . .*

Luke 22:47-48, *NRSV*

THE GOSPEL READING
Luke 22:47-53, *NRSV*

108

THE REFLECTION
THE POWER OF DARKNESS

It has a way of taking control, of stealing our sensibilities, of sending reason out the window and making absurdities seem like normalities. It's the power of the darkness—evil skulking through God's good creation. Take a look! An act of love and affection twisted ever so easily into a signal for betrayal. Deceiving lips pressing forward to devour the agent of God's creating activity.

The disciples get suctioned into the unholy frenzy. Craziness overtakes their volition. Though asking for direction from Jesus, they've no time to wait for a reply. Violence pulses through a hand into a sword and separates an ear from its roots. These men will take charge of the scene—a normal protective response. But unfortunately, it's full of self-assertion and hostility, full of impatience and lack of respect for Christ's power. Had they been praying instead of sleeping, would they have acted differently?

Then there's Jesus! His light bursts forth from the dark patches in Luke's chiaroscuro. He dominates the scene—pointing out the absurdities of the kiss and night-shrouded capture, taking up once more His ministry of healing, halting with one command an unwanted defense. "No more of this!" "Enough!" The only person who understands the implications of the hour knows that the darkness is closing in with claws extended. Resisting it means resisting God's will. The habitual prayers offered in this place have left their mark—have left Him understanding God's plan. The darkness must snuff out His light; this is the hour in which it is allowed to descend—to consume the light.

How often has our hand worked against the purposes of God while we, ill prepared and prayerless, have thought we acted for the good? How many heads have we lopped off in the name of the good? Humility is advised by this story. There is admonition to a renewed prayer life so that we may discern what really needs protection. "No more of this!" No more prayerless rushing forward! We've time to hear what God has to say first, even with darkness all around.

THE BIDDING PRAYER

Help me, Lord Jesus, die to self this day. (silence)
Light of the world, shine into my darkness. (silence)
Jesus, show me how to serve the members of Your Body. (silence)
Enliven my spirit as I reveal myself to You in written word. (silence)

THE JOURNAL

*Later on that day, the disciples had gathered together,
but, fearful of the Jews, had locked all the doors in the house.
Jesus entered, stood among them, and said, "Peace to you."
Then he showed them his hands and side.*

*The disciples, seeing the Master with their own eyes,
were exuberant. Jesus repeated his greeting: "Peace to you.
Just as the Father sent me, I send you."*

*Then he took a deep breath and breathed into them. "Receive the
Holy Spirit," he said. "If you forgive someone's sins, they're gone for
good. If you don't forgive sins, what are you going to do with them?"*

John 20:19-23, *The Message*

THE GOSPEL READING
John 20:19-31, *The Message*

THE REFLECTION
A GENEROUS GOD

What a Sunday evening service the Church got on Christ's resurrection day! The front doors were bolted tight for fear the authorities would shut them down, run them out of town, or worse. Fear was in the air. Then God decided to drop in to liven up the service. Enter Jesus, stage right. (Was it "right"? How *did* He get in there anyway?) Skipping announcement time, He got down to His sermon. (Can you believe it—no announcements?!)

"Peace to you."

Quick . . . snappy . . . to the point . . . I like it. Now, what about an object lesson?

"Yes, this is it—the same body you saw on the cross on Friday. Go ahead, touch it if you like."

Whoa! I've never seen a preacher put it like that *before. Hey, what's he breathing so heavy for?*

"Receive the Holy Spirit."

Look, Peter! It's not even Pentecost, 'n' I got the Spirit!

"Time to get busy taking care of people's sins. I send you into the world!"

Now that *was a good service. What a charge to the congregation. We've got to find Thomas! He'll never believe this.*

This God wants us to experience His resurrection. He's had all of these Gospel accounts written down so we might believe and have eternal life. We're assured of this by Jesus' words directed to us:

"Even better blessings are in store for those who believe without seeing" (John 20:29, *The Message*). It's hard to imagine, but better things are in store for us—better than seeing Him in the flesh, better than having the Spirit breathed from His mouth directly into us. We serve a generous God! It's time to be generous to the world with His message, for He's sending us out too.

THE BIDDING PRAYER

Risen Lord, grant me your peace. (silence)
Christ alive, help me believe. (silence)
Jesus, show me how to feed Your sheep. (silence)
You said, "Surely I am coming soon." I say with the saints, "Come, Lord Jesus!" (silence)

Then the high priest said to him, "I put you under oath before the living
God, tell us if you are the Messiah, the Son of God." Jesus said to him,
"You have said so. But I tell you,
From now on you will see the Son of Man
seated at the right hand of Power
and coming on the clouds of heaven."

Matthew 26:63-64, *NRSV*

THE GOSPEL READING
Matthew 26:56-68, *NRSV*

THE REFLECTION
ALONE, SURROUNDED, AND RULING

We're not given the details, but somehow only Jesus has been seized.
The disciples were either unimportant to His capture or they were
quick to escape from the Garden of Gethsemane. Now Jesus is
alone, and we get a first look at Him surrounded by enemies. It's a
chilling scene: an illegal nighttime trial with a predetermined
course of testimony; political heavyweights silencing a threat to
their power; mocking and violence adopted as tools of justice.

What will this prayer-readied person do as death makes itself a
living threat? *Silence* is the first activity Matthew documents. It's an
action associated with Jesus' prayer life, which continues even

under strain and persecution. Stability of being—it's what we want in ourselves but can only find in this Christ.

Next we're shown Christ using Scripture to respond to His foe, reminiscent of Jesus' confrontation with Satan in the wilderness of Matthew 4, three years earlier. Here Jesus makes reference to a psalm that is definitive for the nation of Israel and the Jewish people. Psalm 110, a David psalm, contains all the messianic hopes of the Jews—reveals the Messiah as conquering king. What an absurdity it must seem to these power brokers that Jesus would apply this Scripture to Himself, in *His* situation. The second verse of this psalm contains the line, "Rule in the midst of your foes" (Psalm 110:2, *RSV*)! "Power to rule? You must be joking!" We can hear the taunting.

And what are we to make of this scene? Alone, surrounded, yet *ruling*? Torture imminent, and *ruling*? Death tomorrow and . . . *ruling*? It doesn't make sense—not in the way that common sense—the world's sense—would lead us to think. Once again we have our God spinning us on our heads. Up is down and down is up. Salvation rule comes in a way that's incomprehensible to humanity. Victory achieved by death.

Christ must walk this road alone, but He walks it for our good—to bring us peace and stability out of the darkness. As Psalm 110:3 affirms:

> Your people will freely join you, resplendent in holy armor
> > on the great day of your conquest,
> Join you at the fresh break of day,
> > join you with all the vigor of youth (*The Message*).

THE BIDDING PRAYER

Help me, Lord Jesus, die to self this day. (silence)
Light of the world, shine into my darkness. (silence)
Jesus, show me how to serve the members of Your Body. (silence)
Enliven my spirit as I reveal myself to You in written word. (silence)

THE JOURNAL

Then Peter remembered what Jesus had said: "Before the cock crows,
you will deny me three times." And he went out and wept bitterly.

Matthew 26:75, *NRSV*

THE GOSPEL READING
Matthew 26:69-75, *NRSV*

THE REFLECTION
WEEPING FOR FAILURE

His is the strongest disposition among the disciples. He's the chosen leader. Bedrock upon which Jesus said He'd build the Church (see Matthew 16:18). *Of course* Peter would be the one who'd follow Jesus to the high priest's house. He's got the guts to try to do something about this situation. Hadn't he said, "Lord, I am ready to go with you to prison and to death" (Luke 22:33, *NRSV*)? It's perilous! If he was let go by the soldiers earlier, they will not give him a second pass. Definitely not; he might be plotting a rescue. The guards would surely seize him, but here he is anyway, regardless of the danger.

It seems daring and commendable even in the light of knowing what will happen. Peter places himself at the brink of decision.

Perhaps he starts after Jesus hoping he could live down the prophecy—maybe prove it wrong. Or perhaps his love gets the better of his reason. He *is,* after all, the disciple who, when Jesus asks three times "Do you love me?" responds thrice "You know that I love you" (John 21, *NRSV*). But here he is, an accusation in his face—"You're one of Jesus' guys!"—and he doesn't stand firm.

There's a reason the prayer that Jesus taught His disciples contains the lines "And lead us not into temptation, but deliver us from evil" (Matthew 6:13, *RSV*). For most often, we disciples find ourselves unable to be the rescuing hero, unable to be the faithful follower, unable to stand firm against something and say, "Yes! I'm for Jesus." Regret and weeping follow us as we run away.

Christ knows this aspect of His disciples, knows our weak wills, knows every act we'll commit, either for or against Him. And still He loves us—was willing to die for us.

So for our part, we pray, "Forgive our sins; lead us not into temptation; deliver us from evil." For our part, sometimes we weep. And for our part, always we get up and return to Kingdom work.

A brother asked Abba Sisoes, "What shall I do, abba, for I have fallen?" The old man said, "Get up again." The brother said, "I have got up again, but have fallen again." The old man said, "Get up again and again." So then the brother said, "How many times?" The old man said, "Until you are either taken up in virtue or in sin. For a man presents himself to judgement in the state in which he is found."[4]

THE BIDDING PRAYER

Help me, Lord Jesus, die to self this day. (silence)
Light of the world, shine into my darkness. (silence)
Jesus, show me how to serve the members of Your Body. (silence)
Enliven my spirit as I reveal myself to You in written word. (silence)

THE JOURNAL

When Judas, his betrayer, saw that Jesus was condemned,
he repented and brought back the thirty pieces of silver to the chief
priests and the elders. He said, "I have sinned by betraying innocent
blood." But they said, "What is that to us? See to it yourself."
Throwing down the pieces of silver in the temple, he departed;
and he went and hanged himself.

Matthew 27:3-5, *NRSV*

THE GOSPEL READING
Matthew 27:1-10, *NRSV*

124

THE REFLECTION
KNOWING WHERE TO RUN

It would be difficult to produce a more damning picture of the religious system of Jesus' day than we have here. Grace, forgiveness, truth, love—all lacking. A person seeking to right a wrong, to offer repentance, finds the spiritual leaders saying, "What do we care? That's *your* problem" (Matthew 27:4, *The Message*)! These supposed holy men, these men of the law send a supplicant to suicide with no compassion, wanting only to keep their hands pristine by getting rid of the blood money. What would have been Judas' story had he run to Jesus instead? This Christ who intercedes for His executioners, praying, "Father, forgive them; for they do not know what they are doing" (Luke 23:34, *NRSV*); this Jesus, who tells a crucified thief that he'll be joining Him in paradise by day's end.

There is no forgiveness and comfort down the path Judas chooses. His desperation appears justified when one considers the Old Testament law (the Torah). Paul, writing to the Romans some years after Judas's death, makes plain that one cannot be redeemed by the law: "For 'no human being will be justified in his sight' by deeds prescribed by the law, for through the law comes the knowledge of sin" (Romans 3:20, *NRSV*). The law offers humanity only the knowledge of sin and the punishment of death. There is nothing our acts can do to save us. Judas's despair is real, is justified. The priests, like any other human being, cannot dispense forgiveness.

Paul goes on to show how hope returns in Christ: "The sacrificed Jesus made us fit for God, set us *right with God*" (Romans 4:25, *The Message*). Here's something Judas's despair robbed him of the chance to see—this Christ who waits for us to return to Him from our places of betrayal, from our sin.

What silvery thing has stolen your attention away from your Lord—tempted you enough to weaken your love for this Jesus? Throw it back wherever it came from but do not forget where to run with your repentance. Jesus—your Lord—says, "I care. Your problems *are* My problems. So much so that I gave My life to take care of them. Run to Me and know that you're already forgiven!"

THE BIDDING PRAYER

Help me, Lord Jesus, die to self this day. (silence)
Light of the world, shine into my darkness. (silence)
Jesus, show me how to serve the members of Your Body. (silence)
Enliven my spirit as I reveal myself to You in written word. (silence)

THE JOURNAL

*Then they took Jesus from Caiaphas to Pilate's headquarters.
It was early in the morning. They themselves did not enter the head-
quarters, so as to avoid ritual defilement and to be able to eat the
Passover. So Pilate went out to them and said . . .*

John 18:28-29, *NRSV*

THE GOSPEL READING
John 18:28-38, *NRSV*

THE REFLECTION
THE UNSEEN KINGDOM

Beating a blasphemer?—Check!—Allowed.
Spitting on a heretic?—Check!—Allowed.
Slapping a deviant?—Check!—Allowed.

So far there's nothing on their interrogation and prosecution check-
list that would defile these "holy men" and keep them from eating
the Passover. But they're not finished with this business yet. They
need to ask the Roman governor his permission to kill their catch,
which means going near Gentile territory. It's got "unclean" written
all over it; they'll have to stay outside the buildings and make their
case from a distance if they want to eat the holy meal later in the day.

Standing outside Gentile headquarters?—Check!—Allowed.

John's description gives us a clearer picture of these so-called holy men. Hands dirtied with abuse and torture are acceptable (i.e., undefiled) but not bodies that have been under a Gentile roof. Wrapped in the law, they're unable to see the absurdities, unable to hear about truth and real purity.

Then there's Pilate, a man given to verbal sparring and dismissive of these Jewish leaders—a man of power, with a storehouse of indifferent questions for would-be challengers. But he's also a man whose mind is trapped in the here and now, bound by the empirical. His mental categories are not broad enough to take in this Christ-from-beyond-the-visible-world. He's a man of facts and tangibles who finds himself in an awkward position: "He does not accept the charges of 'the Jews' but neither will he listen to the voice of Jesus."[5] He understands the spuriousness of the Jews' condemnation but is without the capacity to experience Christ's empyrean kingdom.

Jesus moves with feet in both worlds. He walks among the spiritual legalists tending their checklists, among the world's power-monkeys: "See no Kingdom! Hear no Kingdom! Speak no Kingdom!" All the while, He is testifying to His origins, beckoning to the legalists and the power hungry, saying, "Belong to the truth! Listen to My voice!" even as they torture, abuse and sentence Him to death.

THE BIDDING PRAYER

Help me, Lord Jesus, die to self this day. (silence)
Light of the world, shine into my darkness. (silence)
Jesus, show me how to serve the members of Your Body. (silence)
Enliven my spirit as I reveal myself to You in written word. (silence)

THE JOURNAL

*And when he learned that he was under Herod's jurisdiction,
he sent him off to Herod, who was himself in Jerusalem at that time.
When Herod saw Jesus, he was very glad, for he had been wanting
to see him for a long time, because he had heard about him and was
hoping to see him perform some sign. He questioned him at
some length, but Jesus gave him no answer.*

Luke 23:7-9, *NRSV*

THE GOSPEL READING
Luke 23:4-12, *NRSV*

THE REFLECTION
A SHIFTING FACE

You've seen the face at Christmastime or, perhaps, heard it described in story form.

The Stage:
A gift, which has been anticipated, is on its way; hands are rubbed in the waiting and nerves tingle with the wanting of it. Then the gift arrives and is ripped open with a flurry. All its parts are assembled. Time to test it out, run it through its paces. A face of suspense grins at everything around it.

The Rub:

The gift doesn't meet expectations. In fact, it's not at all what was wanted. And the hands so eagerly rubbed become gift destroyers. The package is cast off, abused. The puppy is whipped, the toy shattered, the sweater laid in the waste bin. A face of frustration glares at anything unlucky to turn its way.

The Face:

It's Herod's mercurial mug—his fickle puss. Pilate sends a present—something Herod has wanted to get his hands on for months, something he thinks will do him a good turn, make miracles erupt, but the gold's not panning; nothing but dross through and through. Happy face turns into torture face. Herod will make this gift pay for being a disappointment, make the puppy dance, pluck the wings from this fly, cram it chock-full o' firecrackers and light the fuse. A darkened face turns on Jesus.

The Gift:

Pilate has it right, at least on one level. There's nothing wrong with the present he sends to Herod. There's no accusation anyone can bring against Jesus that can honestly condemn Him. But Herod misses the significance of the Jesus-gift. He's a gift that must be treated in a new way, opened altogether differently. He requires that we unwrap ourselves as we unwrap Him—stripping off our sin coverings as He unveils layer after layer of His person. What a change of expectations is required to do this! An entirely different kind of face emerges on us! There is no power to amuse a tyrant's ego here, no self-glory to be unpackaged . . . hoarded. Accepting this present means, in the short term, denial and ego-destruction. But ahhhhh! In the long term, hope and life eternal.

Us:
And what will we do with Jesus? How will our expressions change as we tear open this gift during Lent? Jesus is not the package, when unwrapped, that we'll have expected. That's part of His gift to us. For our expectations need redemption along with the rest of our person.

THE BIDDING PRAYER

Help me, Lord Jesus, die to self this day. (silence)
Light of the world, shine into my darkness. (silence)
Jesus, show me how to serve the members of Your Body. (silence)
Enliven my spirit as I reveal myself to You in written word. (silence)

THE JOURNAL

_____

_____

_____

_____

Pilate, wanting to release Jesus, addressed them again;
but they kept shouting, "Crucify, crucify him!"
Luke 23:20-21, *NRSV*

THE GOSPEL READING
Luke 23:13-25, *NRSV*

THE REFLECTION
ENEMY WEEPING

"O Jerusalem, Jerusalem, killing the prophets and stoning those who are sent to you! How often would I have gathered your children together as a hen gathers her brood under her wings, and you would not! Behold your house is forsaken. And I tell you, you will not see me until you say, 'Blessed is he who comes in the name of the Lord!'" (Luke 13:34-35, *RSV*). Jesus spoke these words some months before entering Jerusalem on Palm Sunday—the day on which He looked like a conquering hero to many of the inhabitants. Today's Gospel reading finds Jesus one week after the hosanna-filled Palm Sunday entrance, and many Jerusalemites have awakened in time to chant "Crucify him!" Fickle people, yes; but that's not the real story.

The real story is a Savior weeping for these unreliable people. Before that Palm Sunday entrance, Luke tells us, "And when [Jesus] drew near and saw the city he wept over it, saying, 'Would that even today you knew the things that make for peace! But now they are hid from your eyes'" (Luke 19:41-42, *RSV*). An innocent man—judged so by a Roman governor and a Hebrew king—is in the habit of weeping for a city that will be the death of Him. Guilty of no evil, yet He is willing to die for these, His enemies who know nothing of real peace. Turn the other cheek; love your enemies; pray for your persecutors; be perfect as God is perfect—all of these exhortations from Jesus' sermons get played out in His living, and in His dying.

We live in a time when grace-extending living is not respected. Instead we're told to be "smart" about dealing with our enemies; we're told to be strong in our responses to those who hate our "lifestyles." We're raised to value safety and overpowering defenses. We try to mask the "crucify him" whispers that rise from these activities. Jesus' manner of meeting death is clearly nothing like our way of protecting ourselves. Perhaps we are more like Jerusalem than we know. How would a people live who wept for their enemies, who sacrificed their lives for them? Christ desires to help us discover how, for He is interested in redeeming our minds and our lifestyles.

It's significant that the first place Christ sends His disciples with His resurrection message is Jerusalem: "And you shall be my witnesses in Jerusalem and in all Judea and Samaria and to the end of the earth" (Acts 1:8, *RSV*). He does not give up on these people, but returns in His disciples to offer hope beyond their treachery. This is the Spirit of God, the spirit of forgiveness, mercy and long-suffering. It is a spirit desperately needed in our world and our living. It is the spirit that Jesus is renewing in us as we walk through the darkness.

THE BIDDING PRAYER

Help me, Lord Jesus, die to self this day. (silence)
Light of the world, shine into my darkness. (silence)
Jesus, show me how to serve the members of Your Body. (silence)
Enliven my spirit as I reveal myself to You in written word. (silence)

THE JOURNAL

Meanwhile, the eleven disciples were on their way to Galilee, headed for the mountain Jesus had set for their reunion. The moment they saw him they worshiped him. Some, though, held back, not sure about worship, about risking themselves totally. Jesus, undeterred, went right ahead and gave his charge . . .

Matthew 28:16-18, *The Message*

THE GOSPEL READING
Matthew 28:16-20, *The Message*

THE REFLECTION
FILLING THE EMPTINESS WITHIN

You can't help it—not if you love Him. No sir. If you see Jesus, you fall down or you grab Him and you worship Him. Mary grabs Jesus outside the tomb and doesn't want to let Him go (see John 20:16-17); John sees Him in a revelation and falls "at his feet as though dead" (Revelation 1:17, *NRSV*); Peter, from his boat, sees Jesus onshore and bounds into the sea to get to Him quickly (see John 21:7). Natural responses. These are the kind of actions we're made for— all-or-nothing passion for this God. One long, continuous, shoot-the-wad, bet it-all, never-look-back giving of yourself to Jesus. Why wouldn't we, after what He's given for us?

Well, it's just that there's this little thing we've been unearthing for three weeks: the [self, I, me, it]. (I'll use brackets to indicate this thing we've exposed—this black hole of inward-thinking, consume-everything, fall-down-and-worship-this-direction [self, I, me, it]. I'll use the word "you" to indicate the real being you become as you're filled with Jesus.) [ ] sneaks in after you see Jesus and starts talking dirt. Makes you wonder, "Should I be doing this?" [ ] sparks doubt and hesitation in you. You want to commit but [ ] doesn't want to give up some things—the things [ ] likes. [ ] turns your attention from Jesus and brings with [ ] fear and hesitation like we see from some of the disciples in today's Gospel reading. The *NRSV* reads, "When they saw him, they worshiped him; but some doubt-ed." The Greek word for "doubt" is used in only one other place in the New Testament: when Peter gets out of a boat carrying the dis-ciples and starts walking over storm-tossed waters to meet Jesus who has come walking toward them on the sea (see Matthew 14:22-31). Peter takes his eyes off Jesus and starts to sink; Jesus grabs him and asks, "Why did you doubt?" A wholehearted water-walk to Jesus cut short by [ ] concern. Worship pulled up short.

Jesus knows how to heal this [ ]. Knows how to unbracket it, fill the void, make [ ] into a real self full of *Being*. Jesus gives us a charge. Gets the void directed toward His kingdom again, toward His people, His work. Tells us, "Go! Make disciples! Baptize! Teach! Remember!"

It's good to know that Jesus is undeterred by the emptiness within us. He's the only being who can fill this [ ]—the only person who can draw us out of the [ ] and cause us to worship. And wonderfully, marvelously, He'll keep doing it day after day after day, to the end of the age.

THE BIDDING PRAYER

Risen Lord, grant me Your peace... (silence)
Christ alive, help me believe. (silence)
Jesus, show me how to feed Your sheep. (silence)
You said, "Surely I am coming soon." I say with the saints,
"Come, Lord Jesus!" (silence)

[Pilate] said to the Jews, "Here is your King!" They cried out, "Away with him! Away with him! Crucify him!" Pilate asked them, "Shall I crucify your King?" The chief priests answered, "We have no king but the emperor." Then he handed him over to them to be crucified.

John 19:14-16, *NRSV*

THE GOSPEL READING
John 19:1-16, *NRSV*

THE REFLECTION
TO HUMBLY SERVE A KING

When reading this passage, it's hard to imagine Jesus as High King over anything. His skin is flayed, He has a punching-bag face, thorn-cushion head and is got up like a vaudeville Macbeth. He's a sight worthy of mocking for the Romans, unless they've some moral qualms about taunting the weak. It's understandable that the soldiers use Him as a distraction; they're well trained for such work. Pilate finds no relief from his fears in the presence of this man—he sees no special powers in Jesus. The prisoner is nothing more than an object over which Pilate thinks he exercises full control—an ant in the governor's palm.

How lucky we are to scan this scene in light of God's revelation—to look back in time with the Spirit holding up what is true!

We've committed our lives to "Jesus Christ the faithful witness, the first-born of the dead, and the ruler of kings on earth" (Revelation 1:5, *RSV*). So we understand how wrong-way-round God's methods are from Pilate's position; it's simply incomprehensible to Pilate that this man is a "King" and "Son of God."

That so many people failed to comprehend what God was doing in Jesus should give us pause. We'd have likely missed the significance of this scene had we been walking near the Gabbatha. How much of God's work are we missing as we walk through *our* days? How many of our acts cry out against God's wrong-way-round method—a crowd of one denying the King to whom it has committed? Humility allows us to serve this God and keeps us looking for the strange ways He acts in this world—ways we will not fully comprehend until He returns for us. "For now we see in a mirror dimly, but then face to face. Now I know in part; then I shall understand fully, even as I have been fully understood" (1 Corinthians 13:12, *RSV*).

And when He returns, there will be no mistaking this Jesus: "First of the royal line, High King over all of earth's kings" (Psalm 89:27, *The Message*). A High King who loves but cannot be controlled. A King who—because He appeared before Pilate as He did, because He was condemned, mocked and died—we will see clothed differently one day.

One like a son of man, clothed with a long robe and with a golden girdle round his breast; his head and his hair were white as wool, white as snow; his eyes were like a flame of fire, his feet were like burnished bronze, refined as in a furnace, and his voice was like the sound of many waters; in his right hand he held seven stars, from his mouth issued a sharp two-edged sword, and his face was like the sun shining in full strength. . . . "Fear not, I am the first and the last, and the living one; I died, and behold I am alive for evermore, and I have the keys of Death and Hades" (Revelation 1:13-18, *RSV*).

THE BIDDING PRAYER

Help me, Lord Jesus, die to self this day. (silence)
Light of the world, shine into my darkness. (silence)
Jesus, show me how to serve the members of Your Body. (silence)
Enliven my spirit as I reveal myself to You in written word. (silence)

THE JOURNAL

So when Pilate saw that he could do nothing, but rather that a riot was beginning, he took some water and washed his hands before the crowd, saying, "I am innocent of this man's blood; see to it yourselves." Then the people as a whole answered, "His blood be on us and on our children!" So he released Barabbas for them; and after flogging Jesus, he handed him over to be crucified.

Matthew 27:24-26, *NRSV*

THE GOSPEL READING
Matthew 27:24-26, *NRSV*

THE REFLECTION
SANITIZED

I picked up a leaking pack of chicken today at the grocery store and placed it in my shopping basket. I pulled my hand up feeling a bit contaminated. Really, I've been infected with our society's bacteria-worry-bug. As I looked around, I saw too late the plastic bag and paper towel dispensers on the wall.

Then I had the audacity to place the drippy Styrofoam trays on a cashier's sterilized conveyor belt—moving-infection inching its way rhythmically toward her. But just in time the belt's movement was halted, the packages bagged, and a sanitizer and towels were produced from underneath the checkstand. Whish, whish, whish—

wipe, wipe, wipe—pure again! A slightly forced smile on a tilted head hid all but a trace of a fellow neatnik's annoyance while I contemplated returning to vegetarianism.

Today's Gospel reading shows Jesus being treated like a piece of infected meat. Everyone around Him is trying to sanitize themselves from infection. Pilate doesn't want his name contaminated—he'll not execute an innocent person. "Pass the soft soap; it's hand-washing time!" Whish, whish, whish—scrub, scrub, scrub— "Look, everyone, I'm innocent." The crowd doesn't want to be infected by "heretical" teaching that challenges how they attend to God. "Pass us His blood; we'll bathe in it!" Whish, whish, whish— lather, lather, lather—"Heretic's blood; God will bless us!"

It's not a flattering picture of the human capacity for judging purity. Pilate thinks he's pure and the crowd demented. The crowd thinks they're pure and Jesus evil. All impurities are directed to another party, all purity attributed to one's self. It's a formula oft repeated in our daily living. It's what we get when we forget our sinfulness, forget that we're not freed of responsibility for God's death—not by any means of our own that is. His blood is upon us because our sins require Jesus' death.

Providentially, His blood flows down on us in another, and entirely different, way. For through His death—through the shedding of His blood—our sins no longer condemn us. His blood becomes that which sanitizes, washes us clean, makes us children of God. His death is our atonement. Whish, whish, whish—wipe, wipe, wipe—"Your sins are forgiven!"

We can never be free of this man's blood, and our Lenten journey reminds why none of us should hope to be free of it. For through His sacrifice, Christ has gained the power to make us pure and spotless, freed of sin's contamination, sanitized.

THE BIDDING PRAYER

Help me, Lord Jesus, die to self this day. (silence)
Light of the world, shine into my darkness. (silence)
Jesus, show me how to serve the members of Your Body. (silence)
Enliven my spirit as I reveal myself to You in written word. (silence)

THE JOURNAL

_____

_____

_____

_____

_____

_____

_____

_____

_____

PART FOUR

THE FOURTH
10 DAYS

Then the soldiers led [Jesus] into the courtyard of the palace;
and they called together the whole cohort.

Mark 15:16, *NRSV*

THE GOSPEL READING
Mark 15:16-20, *NRSV*

THE REFLECTION
A LONG JOURNEY, AND ENEMIES ALL AROUND

154

If you're like me, you're at the point where this Lenten journey seems unending. This is the three-quarter mark, with the last and hardest quarter to go. Can we make it to the end? Will our strength be enough? The disciplines we've taken on for this season are getting taxing; we're thinking about the things we've given up more and more often. Spring is coming, tulips are starting to perk up, and we're stuck in death mode—weighted down with crucifixion contemplation. When will it end?

We find Jesus partway through His death march in today's reading. Surrounded by enemies, He can pray David's psalm with no hint of irony:

Yahweh! Look! Enemies past counting!
Enemies sprouting like mushrooms,

Mobs of them all around me, roaring their mockery:
"Hah! No help for *him* from God!" (Psalm 3:1-2, *The Message*).

Three hundred to six hundred soldiers pack in around Jesus in the palace courtyard—an entire cohort ready for duty, popping up with harassments: a purple robe, a thorn crown, mock salutes and counterfeit worship. Today's mission: torture. No reservations—everything sanctioned by the governor and applauded by the people. The soldiers' actions show that they've been attending to the trial enough to know the charge against Jesus. "This man thinks he's *king*? *Wellllll* . . . let's help him be one!" is their response. Christ, surrounded by enemies, is entering the worst stage of His Passion. Will His strength be enough?

We walk this Lenten road surrounded by the same evil. The enemy would have us give up our disciplines, take it easy and come over to its way of thinking. But through our disciplines we're giving ourselves to this Christ—casting ourselves to His help and to nothing else. Can we make it? Yes! Will our strength be enough? No! We take courage, however, for Christ's strength is sufficient. He's already shown that He can withstand these enemies and remain obedient to the will of God.

Our journey may have been rocky so far; it may get rockier still. We may find ourselves drifting from God's path, but we focus on Jesus. Real help comes from Him; real help comes from God. We can sing David's psalm in the midst of these enemies. We sing it with Christ, who in His mercy guards us all round:

But you, Yahweh, shield me on all sides;
You ground my feet, you lift my head high;
With all my might I shout up to Yahweh,
His answers thunder from the holy mountain.

I stretch myself out. I sleep.
Then I'm up again—rested, tall and steady,
Fearless before the enemy mobs
Coming at me from all sides.

Up, Yahweh! My God, help me!
Slap their faces,
First this cheek, then the other
Your fist hard in their teeth!

Real help comes from Yahweh.
Your blessing clothes your people!
(Psalm 3:3-8, *The Message*).

THE BIDDING PRAYER

Help me, Lord Jesus, die to self this day. (silence)
Light of the world, shine into my darkness. (silence)
Jesus, show me how to serve the members of Your Body. (silence)
Enliven my spirit as I reveal myself to You in written word. (silence)

THE JOURNAL

*As they led [Jesus] away, they seized a man, Simon of Cyrene,
who was coming from the country, and they laid the cross on him,
and made him carry it behind Jesus. A great number of the people
followed him, and among them were women who were beating
their breasts and wailing for him. But Jesus turned to them
and said, "Daughters of Jerusalem, do not weep for me,
but weep for yourselves and for your children."*

Luke 23:26-28, *NRSV*

THE GOSPEL READING
Luke 23:26-31, *NRSV*

THE REFLECTION
DYING RIGHT

Weight . . . burden . . . hardship! Get near this death march and
you're given a bucket-load of troubles; you can't get away unencum-
bered. Simon and the women of Jerusalem get nothing but a cross
and woes in their encounters with Jesus. "Weep for yourselves!"—at
least Jesus is giving them straight talk! No sugarcoating it here.
In his word picture of Simon, Luke is reminding his readers of
Jesus' words to the crowds earlier in His ministry: "Whoever does
not carry the cross and follow me cannot be my disciple . . . none of

you can become my disciple if you do not give up all your possessions" (Luke 14:27,33, *NRSV*). Lay down everything you've prided yourself on possessing in this life and step forward to pick up your lethal injection. Time to die!

There are two types of death and pain at work in these encounters: that which is from below and that which is from above; one devoid of hope and one offering hope only through hardness. We've been looking at the former type as we've studied characters in the Passion. Judas finding no forgiveness; chief priests doling out hatred and execution; a crowd longing to see crucifixion; soldiers mocking, torturing and now conscripting Simon. These characters exemplify a pain and death with no hope, no light arising from it. Suicide Judas-style provides an apt portrait of this path; no one to restore us, no one to forgive us—only blackness and despair.

Then there's Christ, whose Passion march represents another type of pain and dying. This Son of Man, this God, urges us to pick up His type of death, His type of suffering, and follow. He says that we must die to that part of our self that destroys and whose grip is so tight that releasing it seems like death eternal. We're asked to turn our self to ash, sacrifice its desires and controls and trust that Christ can fill its empty space.

There is not the option of choosing life or death. One's only choice is choosing the right way to die. One death march leads *only* to death; the other leads to a suffering death like our Lord's. But out of this second death march comes newness of life! Only the Jesus-path finds us rising from the ashes.

Remember, you are dust and to dust you shall return!
Oh yes, we *will* die.
So let us choose the right way to do it.
Descend into the darkness with Jesus!

THE BIDDING PRAYER

Help me, Lord Jesus, die to self this day. (silence)
Light of the world, shine into my darkness. (silence)
Jesus, show me how to serve the members of Your Body. (silence)
Enliven my spirit as I reveal myself to You in written word. (silence)

THE JOURNAL

_____

_____

_____

_____

_____

_____

_____

_____

In the same way the chief priests, along with the scribes, were also mocking him among themselves and saying, "He saved others; he cannot save himself. Let the Messiah, the King of Israel, come down from the cross now, so that we may see and believe." Those who were crucified with him also taunted him.

Mark 15:31-32, *NRSV*

THE GOSPEL READING
Mark 15:25-32, *NRSV*

162

THE REFLECTION
OXYMORONIC SALVATION

It's oxymoronic salvation they're calling for—this save-yourself thinking. "Get yourself down from *there* why don't you . . . ha-ha-ha." There's an illogically evil vein running unseen through their thinking, which when exposed will crumble, taking along with it their smug worlds. You see, all these mockers have come to depend upon themselves, and they expect that any truly strong person will do the same. Strong religious minds will keep religious laws and stand firmly behind systems that enforce them. Strong soldiers will get the better of enemies of the state who oppose them, or die fighting—finishing strong. Strong criminals will be full of contempt for others and show their strength by resisting other wills.

Deride the infidels, crush enemies, taunt the weak. Stir these three together and you'd get one nasty-to-be-around person. This kind of person would consume you, run you down, crush you if he got the chance. Not much of a thing from which to be seeking salvation. Still such a person does *seem* able to save himself or herself.

But it's not *really* true, and there's the rub. Though this person might seem strong, might carry the world on his back, it cannot last. The long-term view shows the impossibility of anyone's saving himself or herself. Sure, we get out of jams from time to time. But salvation? If you eventually need saving, then salvation is not your forte, you're not the *sine qua non* of salvation. Reckoning time stalks you in the form of disease, accidents, stronger enemies or a face-to-face confrontation with the living God.

We see Jesus against this backdrop in a new way. He is able to offer salvation only if His activities on Earth are never jeopardized by events or people around Him; only if there are no instances where saving Him is necessitated. And He's already told us that this is true of His death march. He's come to this place of crucifixion by His own power and by the will of God. Having cast Himself into the Father's hands, He trusts that His death will not be final—that resurrection is accomplished in the Trinity.

Many voices are still offering up empty salvation, telling us to save ourselves. It takes strength to admit this is not possible. It takes daily surrender to the will of God, daily rejection of the voices to "be strong!"

Remember the words of Saint Paul, a strong man of the world struck blind by God in order to save his soul: "Isn't it obvious that God deliberately chose men and women that the culture overlooks and exploits and abuses, chose these 'nobodies' to expose the hollow pretensions of the 'somebodies'? That makes it quite clear that none of you can get by with blowing your own horn before God" (1 Corinthians 1:27-28, *The Message*).

THE BIDDING PRAYER

Help me, Lord Jesus, die to self this day. (silence)
Light of the world, shine into my darkness. (silence)
Jesus, show me how to serve the members of Your Body. (silence)
Enliven my spirit as I reveal myself to You in written word. (silence)

THE JOURNAL

Then the chief priests of the Jews said to Pilate, "Do not write,
'The King of the Jews,' but, 'This man said, I am King of the Jews.'"
Pilate answered, "What I have written I have written."

John 19:21-22, *NRSV*

THE GOSPEL READING
John 19:16-22, *NRSV*

THE REFLECTION
BEYOND QUALIFICATION

We're in the habit of qualifying our words and their meanings to suit our purposes. We twist meanings to put ourselves in a good light and to discount other people's work, looks or intelligence. Here are a couple of examples:

"She's *pretty* . . . yes; but then she's rich enough to have someone fix all her blemishes."

"It's a *nice piece of work*. Really though, *anyone* could do it if they had the time."

The chief priests and the Jews have no problem using qualifiers, especially now that they're feeling humiliated by Pilate's placard. They want the governor to qualify what he's written about Jesus, to change the inscription. It's an obvious mistake to them. "Get it modified or we'll be laughingstocks!" Unfortunately for them, they've pushed and pushed Pilate, gotten him to execute a man he thought innocent and made him publicly concede to a demanding crowd. Pilate's ready to thumb his nose at these people: "You don't like what I wrote? Tough! Get *outta* here. I'll not change a thing."

What Pilate and the Jews do not understand, however, is that they have no power to change the situation. Jesus' status as High King cannot be altered; no qualifications are possible that would limit His position—whether in word or in being. God has made sure that Jesus is identified correctly as He dies. Pilate (who thinks he's nose-thumbing these Jews) is used by God to proclaim Jesus' coronation. As Jesus is raised to die, He's acquiring His royal kingdom. It's there for all to see, in three languages no less!

"The real enthronement comes now on the cross when the kingship of Jesus is acknowledged by heraldic proclamation ordered by a representative of the greatest political power on earth and phrased in the sacred and secular languages of the time."[6] It's not qualification time, not limiting or modifying time. We cannot circumscribe this Christ! Instead, it's time to explode worldviews and rearrange our ways of ordering things. Time to see how unmanageable this Jesus really is.

The apostle John affirms in his Revelation what his Gospel account reveals that these Jewish leaders have missed. This really *is* the King of the Jews who is hung out to die. Jesus, "the lion of the tribe of Judah" (Revelation 5:5, *NRSV*), the "King of kings and Lord of lords" (Revelation 19:16, *NRSV*), is being given a coronation that bursts asunder our thoughts of royalty. Here is a king whose crowning comes through death. What an unruly business! A God who cannot be contained and is beyond qualification. C. S. Lewis was right! This Jesus, "He's wild, you know. Not like a *tame* lion."[7]

THE BIDDING PRAYER

Help me, Lord Jesus, die to self this day. (silence)
Light of the world, shine into my darkness. (silence)
Jesus, show me how to serve the members of Your Body. (silence)
Enliven my spirit as I reveal myself to You in written word. (silence)

THE JOURNAL

Jesus said, "Breakfast is ready." Not one of the disciples dared ask,
"Who are you?" They knew it was the Master.
Jesus then took the bread and gave it to them. He did the same
with the fish. This was now the third time Jesus had shown himself
alive to the disciples since being raised from the dead.
After breakfast, Jesus said to Simon Peter, "Simon, son of John,
do you love me more than these?"
"Yes, Master, you know I love you."
Jesus said, "Feed my lambs."

170

He then asked a second time, "Simon, son of John, do you love me?"
"Yes, Master, you know I love you."
Jesus said, "Shepherd my sheep."
Then he said it a third time: "Simon, son of John, do you love me?"
Peter was upset that he asked for the third time,
"Do you love me?" so he answered, "Master, you know everything
there is to know. You've got to know that I love you."
Jesus said, "Feed my sheep."

John 21:12-17, *The Message*

THE GOSPEL READING
John 21:1-25, *The Message*.

THE REFLECTION
A JESUS-MEAL

A group of fishermen—big working men marinated in fish oil, sea salt and hard work—is being seined . . . hauled to shore . . . caught by this Jesus. The bait? Breakfast! They've been working all night with nothing to show for it, and the sun rises on a morning feast. Peter jumps out of the boat he's so excited to get a taste of this food. It's a dish he loves. The other disciples get to shore double-quick and hear the invitation: "Breakfast is ready."

Here it is: fish frying and baked bread cooling. Jesus serves them food to eat, but the scene is infused with a deeper feast. Fish and bread aren't what they've rushed for, nor are fish and bread what Jesus wants to stuff them full of. These everyday rations point to something deeper and more real. He's the meal on which they want to feast, this Jesus is the bread and wine they've eaten before and which they cannot live without. His body broken, His blood poured out—raised from the dead and alive. A meal to fill a burly fisherman's soul.

Filled up on their Jesus-meal, saturated with Christ, they're asked about love. He's filled them with it because He *is* it through 'n' through—divine love. What's to be done with the surfeit? Jesus gives commands: "Follow me" and "Feed my sheep." Breakfast is over, they're full of Jesus and it's time to duplicate this in the lives of others. Call people in from their labors, cook them a meal and feed them the living God—fill them with the love of Jesus. Eat Jesus, follow Jesus, feed people Jesus! May Christ give us the strength to continue this work—to pull up to the table, eat a Jesus-meal and then serve ourselves to another.

THE BIDDING PRAYER

Risen Lord, grant me Your peace. (silence)
Christ alive, help me believe. (silence)
Jesus, show me how to feed Your sheep. (silence)
You said, "Surely I am coming soon." I say with the saints,
"Come, Lord Jesus!" (silence)

This was to fulfill what the scripture says,
"They divided my clothes among themselves,
and for my clothing they cast lots."
And that is what the soldiers did.
Meanwhile, standing near the cross of Jesus were his mother,
and his mother's sister, Mary the wife of Clopas, and Mary Magdalene.
When Jesus saw his mother and the disciple whom he loved standing
beside her, he said to his mother, "Woman, here is your son."
Then he said to the disciple, "Here is your mother." And from
that hour the disciple took her into his own home.

John 19:24-27, *NRSV*

174

THE GOSPEL READING
John 19:23-27, *NRSV*

THE REFLECTION
STRIPPED BUT LOVING

We see God being stripped on two levels in today's reading. God the
Father is being stripped of His "only begotten son," soldier-tormentors
having nailed and raised Him on a cross of wood. Darkness will reach
over the earth (see Matthew 27:45) in apprehension of death's piceous
hold on Jesus' body. This Son, upon whom God the Father looked and

said, "This is my beloved Son, with whom I am well pleased," must suffer and die.

At another level we see God the Son being stripped of His earthly possessions: garments and cloak. Soldier-tormentors have taken everything, and He hangs like a cleated piece of meat. In this condition, He must strip Himself of mother and strip Himself of human sonship as He turns into death's darkness. He must cast Himself into the will of the Father, trusting in God's providence.

All of this is bleak. Watching aggressors wrench belongings from another human being or hearing of a person being forcibly stripped reminds us of all the cruel acts we've experienced in this life. We look around and wonder when the hammer will strike! How can the center hold? When will a robber enter? When will the next death occur? When will health fail? Who will reject their faith? Depression waits like a barista wanting to mix us a confusion-drink.

Yet even with the world doing its best to undo Him, God shows us what is real, shows us how to work in the darkness. God the Father puts boundaries on the activities of these soldiers so that they are in line with His redemptive plan. Scripture is fulfilled so that the Son's work accomplishes all that has been foretold of it. The Father walks through this hour with the Son, working His will in Jesus' last breath and death.

Then we see Jesus! Though pinned down like a sadistic experiment, He attends to this woman who bore Him into the world. He will not leave her barren and childless but entrusts her to this man He greatly loves. Jesus' attentions are turned outwardly as death approaches.

God shows us a way of living, a way of facing death, that all need to see. It lets us shake off depression, spit out the dregs of its black drink and return to God's work. Walking in the darkness we follow the example of our God—loving those who are given to us.

THE BIDDING PRAYER

Help me, Lord Jesus, die to self this day. (silence)
Light of the world, shine into my darkness. (silence)
Jesus, show me how to serve the members of Your Body. (silence)
Enliven my spirit as I reveal myself to You in written word. (silence)

THE JOURNAL

_____

_____

_____

_____

_____

_____

_____

One of the criminals who were hanged there kept deriding him and saying, "Are you not the Messiah? Save yourself and us!" But the other rebuked him, saying, "Do you not fear God. . . ." Then he said, "Jesus, remember me when you come into your kingdom." He replied, "Truly I tell you, today you will be with me in Paradise."

Luke 23:39-40,43, *NRSV*

THE GOSPEL READING
Luke 23:39-43, *NRSV*

THE REFLECTION
PARADISE AT FULL PRICE

We think we know what it would take—we know how we'd arrange things if only we had the power. Scratchless furniture, ding-free cars, nonwrinkly bodies, disease-free brains, plenty of the good life to go around. There's no end to the images we construct that point to this life. Sometimes I walk around the house singing the dream songs "If I Were a Rich Man" or "Wouldn't It Be Lovely":

> Lots of chocolate for me to eat.
> Lots of coal making lots of heat,
> Warm face, warm hands, warm feet.
> Oh, wouldn't it be loverly.[8]

Oh yes, it'd be lovely. Too bad the dream rams us against a problem. You see, we want this loverly life on the cheap; the easy, hardships-removed, cash-'n'-carry paradise is ingrained in our appetitive self. It's what the first criminal in today's reading wants from Jesus. He wants somebody to get him off the cross without regard to the justness of it, without regard to paying for what he's done. It's good to see that seeking the easy path is not just a modern problem. Though our advertising-saturated psyches reveal themselves as experts on this theme, criminal number one reminds us that this is a fundamental human problem.

Matthew and Mark report that criminal number two also derides Jesus while on the cross (see Matthew 27:44; Mark 15:32). Could it be that this criminal gets a clearer picture of reality as the day goes on? Jesus, who bears the taunting and insults without lashing out, affects this dying man. He turns into a Jesus-defender, speaking out to deflect unfounded insults. A criminal starts to see clearly, to see eternal truth bursting through tangible misery, to understand how one can really enter paradise.

We catch glimpses of the real paradise in the everyday; we find hints of it in great literature and music, in science and mathematics. Expressions of order, beauty, truth and love show us its shadows as we walk in a broken world. And then we see Jesus! See Him as this criminal did: hanging near death, sinless, kingly. We turn our gaze on Him as we walk toward death. All other things become secondary. For in this Christ we find paradise reality. It is paradise at full price, a cost paid by Him through His death. And this paradise is offered because He regards us mercifully—we who ask to be in relationship with Him.

Here is that paradise we seek above all the crumbling, scratched and diseased objects of this world—eternity in the company of this perfect being, Jesus.

THE BIDDING PRAYER

Help me, Lord Jesus, die to self this day. (silence)
Light of the world, shine into my darkness. (silence)
Jesus, show me how to serve the members of Your Body. (silence)
Enliven my spirit as I reveal myself to You in written word. (silence)

THE JOURNAL

_____

_____

_____

_____

_____

_____

_____

_____

Then Jesus gave a loud cry and breathed his last. And the curtain of the temple was torn in two, from top to bottom. Now when the centurion, who stood facing him, saw that in this way he breathed his last, he said, "Truly this man was God's Son!"

There were also women looking on from a distance . . .

Mark 15:37-40, *NRSV*

THE GOSPEL READING
Mark 15:33-41, *NRSV*

THE REFLECTION
A FINAL BREATH IN THE DARK

Inky black clouds surround all levels of the world as Jesus draws and exhales His final breaths. Physical creation is covered with darkness; religious spaces are blackened, shaken and torn; the powerful stand gloomily below their death-work, encased by it; and the weak, at a distance as always the weak are forced to be—in the cheap seats even for capital punishments—cannot escape the barrenness. *Tenebrae*, this final darkness of Jesus' death march, is descending in fullness. An unholy eclipse seen at the umbra, with Jesus, the light of the world, forcing out loud cries to His Father. Six weeks from Ash Wednesday we see where our death march has led us.

Jesus wrestles against this darkness. The weight of a history-encompassing evil pushes down and squeezes from Him cries of pain, cries of abandonment, prayer cries. He began His death march with prayer at Gethsemane and ends it with the prayer "My God, my God, why have you forsaken me?" An old psalter prayer, memorized perhaps in youth, issues from His lips at the end. It is a psalm about Him, with lines He would know intimately; for they speak of this scene—"They pin me down hand and foot . . . and then throw dice for my clothes" (Psalm 22:16,18, *The Message*). It is also a psalm that, without minimizing present sufferings, looks ahead to God's restoration.

Though dying, this man knows who His Father is and understands the separation that engulfs Him. It is for us that this is happening—"For our sake he made him to be sin who knew no sin, so that in him we might become the righteousness of God" (2 Corinthians 5:21, *RSV*). Christ must walk away from His Father, having become our sin, so that through death He might be able to save us. An exhale into the dark; the human corpse of God; salvation opened to us. We cannot help but say with the powerful centurion: "Truly this man was God's Son!"

Women who served and waited upon Jesus for years must stand on the sidelines and watch death take Him: a solitary, lonely and empty death. We, and all of humanity, stand with these women—we stand this fight out. The person through whom all things were created and in whom all things exist, the person through whom the breath of life came into our world is losing His breath that we might breathe eternally. All of our Lenten practices and attention point us to this event: the death of God. A final breath into the darkness, which ensures that we will breathe again.[9]

THE BIDDING PRAYER

Help me, Lord Jesus, die to self this day. (silence)
Light of the world, shine into my darkness. (silence)
Jesus, show me how to serve the members of Your Body. (silence)
Enliven my spirit as I reveal myself to You in written word. (silence)

THE JOURNAL

*The Jews did not want the bodies left on the cross during the sabbath,
especially because that sabbath was a day of great solemnity. So they
asked Pilate to have the legs of the crucified men broken and the bodies
removed. Then the soldiers came and broke the legs of the first and of the
other who had been crucified with him. But when they came to Jesus
and saw that he was already dead, they did not break his legs.*

John 19:31-33, *NRSV*

THE GOSPEL READING
John 19:31-37, *NRSV*

THE REFLECTION
UNBROKEN

"Da Sabbath is coming, so we wants you to take care of dis little
problem for us. Capeesh?" It's like reading from a mafioso diary.
"We needs a coupl'a legs broken before dinner. You gotta whack dis
guy!" These men who've received almost everything they've asked
from Pilate need to get the mess cleaned up before dinner; otherwise
it will ruin their holy day. "A day of great solemnity" starts at sun-
down and these men need to be attending to spiritual matters. "So
could we hurry dis dying bit up? We can't have dead bodies hangin'
around tonight." The dealers of death and brokenness have spoken.

Everything of this world either is broken or is going to be broken: toys, machines, houses, minds, emotions, bodies and entire lives. There are forces of evil making this so. Some people choose to align themselves with these forces, to give in to the smashing, breaking tendencies within themselves. They become destroyers. Today's Scripture gives a clear picture of such people. Though it was deemed a mercy to break the legs of one who was crucified (the act hastens death), there is nothing of mercy in these attitudes. These are people who want a man's legacy demolished, encased in stone and buried for good. A spiritual insurrection needs trouncing. Here are destroyers who keep themselves in power using fear and death.

God protects Christ from these men even as His body hangs limp. Death is allowed, but not breaking. These men who fear being defiled by a corpse hanging overnight will not be allowed to defile God by breaking the Son's body. Scripture is fulfilled and God's providence continues: "Many are the afflictions of the righteous, but the Lord rescues them from them all. He keeps all their bones; not one of them will be broken. . . . The Lord redeems the life of his servants" (Psalm 34:19-20,22, *NRSV*). God's work remains unbroken.

We've joined in this fight against the forces of destruction and meet the battle within and without. Christ's death-work means we'll never be forever lost in this battle, though we'll continue to struggle with parts of ourselves that resist Him. It gives us strength to know He has already carried all of our sin—all the muck we uncover in ourselves. He has already died with these things upon His back, so whatever we place upon Him cannot break Him. None of our sins can annihilate His love for us. He remains forever unbroken and ready to mend what is broken in us.

THE BIDDING PRAYER

Help me, Lord Jesus, die to self this day. (silence)
Light of the world, shine into my darkness. (silence)
Jesus, show me how to serve the members of Your Body. (silence)
Enliven my spirit as I reveal myself to You in written word. (silence)

THE JOURNAL

Joseph of Arimathea, a respected member of the council,
who was also himself waiting expectantly for the kingdom of God,
went boldly to Pilate and asked for the body of Jesus.

Mark 15:43, *NRSV*

THE GOSPEL READING
Mark 15:42-46, NRSV

THE REFLECTION
WAITING . . . EXPECTANT . . . READY

Funerals are tough under the best of circumstances. I've been a participant in a number of them, and it takes time to work out the logistics of the service and burial. Our culture carries out funerals on a business model, with retail centers to purchase all the options and professionals to help you get a body buried. But rarely are matters accomplished smoothly even in this professional setting. Funeral directors and ministers find themselves drawn into the orbits of odd personal relationships among people. I've seen pallbearers picked from obscure branches of the family tree just to fill a spot—bearers who care little for respectful attire and solemn observance. On one occasion, I watched a casket almost dropped to the ground by an inattentive distant cousin being too casual about his burial work. We hope our funerals will be solid affairs where proper respect is shown for us and celebration of God happens. But it takes good people who love us to pull this off.

Here's Joseph of Arimathea, Jesus' pallbearer and funeral director. He is a rich man (see Matthew 27:57), a member of the Jewish council, a man who knows how to work within the religious and political systems of his time. He's a bold, get-it-done fellow with a plan whose material aspects are already worked out. He has a way to retrieve, transport and bury the body. What more could Jesus want?

How about a man "waiting expectantly for the kingdom of God"? A man who believes in Jesus and wants His body treated with respect. No dropping of the corpse will be tolerated! A rich man opens his fortune to buy fine linens and a new tomb for this man he has loved. Joseph, a man expectant and prepared, is being used by God to wait upon Jesus.

God grants each of Jesus' followers a place to use their talents. Often it is not the place we would have created had we been free to write our story. Often we think our place unglamorous or unfulfilling. Yet in each of these separate places, God is working something important. We are called to ready ourselves to serve Jesus in order that we might boldly run to His assistance. We sharpen the talents we've been given, often without knowing what God will be doing with them. When the need arises, God will put us to work, for He has a place where we all can be the bold go-to person.

THE BIDDING PRAYER

As we remember this day the work of Joseph, grant us strength, dear God, to sharpen our skills for Jesus. Help us, dear Lord, not to be a distant cousin, unprepared for the work You have for us—someone who'd drop You for lack of attention. Instead, make us like Joseph: expectant, bold and ready for service!

Help me, Lord Jesus, die to self this day. (silence)
Light of the world, shine into my darkness. (silence)
Jesus, show me how to serve the members of Your Body. (silence)
Enliven my spirit as I reveal myself to You in written word. (silence)

THE JOURNAL

The next day, that is, after the day of Preparation, the chief priests and the Pharisees gathered before Pilate and said, "Sir, we remember what that impostor said while he was still alive, 'After three days I will rise again.' Therefore command the tomb to be made secure until the third day; otherwise his disciples may go and steal him away, and tell the people, 'He has been raised from the dead,' and the last deception would be worse than the first." Pilate said to them, "You have a guard of soldiers; go, make it as secure as you can." So they went with the guard and made the tomb secure by sealing the stone.

Matthew 27:62-66, *NRSV*

THE GOSPEL READING
Matthew 27:62-66, *NRSV*

THE REFLECTION
FORGETTING ANYTHING?

Dead and still a threat! The Pharisees understand the power of Jesus though they fail to understand His nature. He succeeded in capturing the spiritual imagination of the people, providing them a view of a God who frees people instead of enslaving them to religious duties. Eliminating His life is not enough to stamp out His threat; now they need to control His corpse and control the news surrounding His death. We're looking at propagandists who want to control any opposition news; information manipulators who've taken charge of the Jewish people's spirituality, treating them like babies who must be spoon-fed without regard for personal discernment. Control the tomb, control the news, control Jesus. Simple formula.

Matthew's Gospel shows how skillful these people are at their game. They've been astute information gatherers and have tuned in to the key component of Jesus' message: "After three days I will rise again." Without this, everything else is a wash, a passing fad, a nonthreat. The disciples haven't even understood this part of the message and here are His enemies worried about the prophecy, about a Savior's promise. So we've the awkward situation in which "the opponents took Jesus' words about rising from the dead more seriously than did the disciples."[10] It's a situation that only heightens the extent to which Jesus fights in solitude this battle for our salvation. His followers are not out implementing a PR campaign, not out pitching the Savior's tomb-opening celebration. They're in hiding—dressed in mourning cloth. And God? He's on His feet fighting for us—continuing to slug it out with Evil, whose forces want the nails pounded deeper into His Son.

The Pharisees? Simple formula. Simple solution. "Like the guy said, 'It's finished,' right? Nothing more to worry about. Guards at the tomb. Are we forgetting anything?"

Resurrection is coming. We know it. We've waited for it. Our Lenten journey is still preparing us to receive the news tomorrow morning. "He is risen. He is risen indeed!" But today we wait and understand how deeply the nails are embedded and how ridiculous Evil will look when Christ is raised.

A tomb sealed? A corpse controlled? Jesus silenced? Forgetting anything? Tomorrow's news will tell!

THE BIDDING PRAYER

Help me, Lord Jesus, die to self this day. (silence)
Light of the world, shine into my darkness. (silence)
Jesus, show me how to serve the members of Your Body. (silence)
Enliven my spirit as I reveal myself to You in written word. (silence)

THE JOURNAL

_____
_____
_____
_____
_____
_____
_____
_____
_____
_____

Then he said, "Everything I told you while I was with you comes to this: All the things written about me in the Law of Moses, in the Prophets, and in the Psalms have to be fulfilled."

He went on to open their understanding of the Word of God, showing them how to read their Bibles this way. He said, "You can see now how it is written that the Messiah suffers, rises from the dead on the third day, and then a total life-change through the forgiveness of sins is proclaimed in his name to all nations—starting from here, from Jerusalem! You're the first to hear and see it. You're the witnesses."

Luke 24:44-48, *The Message*

THE GOSPEL READING
Luke 24:44-48, *The Message*

THE REFLECTION
THAT'S RIGHT . . . US!

HE IS RISEN! JESUS IS RISEN INDEED!
The headlines are out and Evil is on the run. Salvation is open to all who will receive Jesus' gift. There's a tomb busted open, a corpse missing—alive no less—with the news spreading that resurrection from the dead is a reality! The Jewish religious establishment is in

turmoil, not having been able to control the situation. They're fabricating a cover story, putting their spin on the scene, hoping they can put this Messiah back in the grave (see Matthew 28:11-15). But alas, He's walking around telling His followers all about His salvation message!

You can't keep a good God in the grave. Simple formulae, simple solutions—they don't work against this kind of love. His attributes expand in the face of Evil; His person fills the void of nothingness with love, goodness, truth, light, beauty. Mocking torture, brutality and a violent death made God's character shine. What was Jesus doing as the worst was heaped upon Him? Praying, truth-speaking, caring for those around Him, forgiving His enemies. How could anyone imagine that Evil could overcome such character? We shout John's Gospel words: "The light shines in the darkness, and the darkness has not overcome it" (John 1:5, *RSV*).

Easter is here and our Lenten journey over. Or is it? In His resurrection sermon, Jesus is telling His disciples (telling us) to enter anew His work. Shake off our sleepyhead inattentiveness and faithless running away. Shake off our death-depression and inertia. Proclamation of the Gospel is granted to our mouths, to our lives. Speak the truth to all nations, He commands. Tell our neighbors, tell our world: God is alive; Jesus is risen!

That's right—*us*! We're the witnesses. Get up. Don't wait for anything. Run from the empty tomb and tell someone about the love of Jesus.

THE BIDDING PRAYER

Risen Lord, grant me Your peace. (silence)
Christ alive, help me believe. (silence)
Jesus, show me how to feed Your sheep. (silence)
You said, "Surely I am coming soon." I say with the saints, "Come,
Lord Jesus!" (silence)

PASSIONATE LIVING

Here we are, a day or so after Easter, basking in the warmth of Jesus' resurrection light. The sun is warming the northern part of the planet as the earth advances in its orbit. We find ourselves working in the garden, smelling the tulips and dancing in the grass as it starts to green. Our Lenten death march has found its end in Christ's work. Death turns to new life.

We're enlivened by this man who shows us what an obedient journey to death can yield: life—for Christ and all who'll follow Him. An emptied self becomes the fertile field onto which the fullness of God's being springs. An emptied self becomes the model for right living—for the truly passionate journey. It's confusing and invigorating at the same time. It's this upside-down, topsy-turvy, inverted-spirit way of being to which Christ calls us.

Our Lenten preparation has set us in the starting blocks ready to run forward. As the Spirit of God pulls the trigger on the starter's gun, we remember that passion comes in many forms. The past 40-plus days, we've seen what a jumble of conflicting passions, what a mess of appetites and desires we are. We've focused our attention on the person of Jesus, knowing His selfless existence can show us those things about which we must be truly passionate. And while we know we'll not always choose the best things in this life—for our self continues to stumble about wanting its own way—we know this Christ will not leave us flat on our faces but will pick us up when we've fallen.

We know it! We've seen His mercy on our Lenten journey and we're ready to burst out into spring. Ready to tell everyone about Jesus, our true love.

You've all year to run. You've every Sunday to celebrate resurrection. Fifty-two run-from-the-tomb, explode-into-joyous-song, new-birth-celebration days spaced evenly throughout the year. Fifty-two days to stand up as the Gospel is read and attest to the miracle of the empty tomb. Fifty-two days to bear-hug this Jesus and say, "You're alive? I can't believe how lucky I am!"

A LENTEN LITANY FOR SMALL GROUPS

"Remember, you are dust and to dust you shall return!"
Words for the imposition of the ashes—Ash Wednesday

I. Unison Opening Prayer

All:
Lord, silence in us all voices but Your own,
That in hearing we may believe,
And in believing we may obey,
To the glory of Your name.

II. A Canticle of Lamentation (Jeremiah 14:17-21, *NRSV*)

Leader:
God, come to our aid.
O Lord, make haste to help us.

All:
Let my eyes run down with tears night and day, and let
    them not cease,

for the virgin daughter—my people—is struck down with
   a crushing blow, with a very grievous wound.

If I go out into the field, look—those killed by the sword!
And if I enter the city, look—those sick with famine!

For both prophet and priest ply their trade throughout the
   land,
and have no knowledge.

Have you completely rejected Judah? Does your heart
   loathe Zion?

Why have you struck us down so that there is no healing for us?
We look for peace, but find no good; for a time of healing,
   but there is terror instead.

We acknowledge our wickedness, O Lord, the iniquity of
   our ancestors,
for we have sinned against you.

Do not spurn us, for your name's sake; do not dishonor your
   glorious throne;
remember and do not break your covenant with us.

III. Discussion of the Week's Reading

IV. Psalmody (Psalm 130:1-8, *The Message*)

Leader:
God, come to our aid.
O Lord, make haste to help us.

All:
Help, Yahweh—the bottom has fallen out of my life!
    Master, hear my cry for help!
Listen hard! Open your ears!
    Listen to my cries for mercy.

If you, Yahweh, kept records on wrongdoings,
    who would stand a chance?
As it turns out, forgiveness is your habit,
    and that's why you're worshiped.

I pray to Yahweh—my life a prayer—
    and wait for what he'll say and do.

My life's on the line before God, my Lord,
    waiting and watching till morning,
    waiting and watching till morning.

Oh Israel, wait and watch for Yahweh—
    with Yahweh's arrival comes love,
    with Yahweh's arrival comes generous redemption.

No doubt about it—he'll redeem Israel,
buy back Israel from captivity to sin.

V. Silence (5-plus minutes)

VI. Benediction: Simeon's Song—*Nunc Dimittis* (Luke 2:29-32, *The Message*)

All:
God, you can now release your servant;
release me in peace as you promised.
With my own eyes I've seen your salvation;
it's now out in the open for everyone to see:
A God-revealing light to the non-Jewish nations,
and of glory for your people Israel.

VII. Announcements and Prayer Requests

ENDNOTES

1. Rainer Maria Rilke, *Letters to a Young Poet* (Classic Wisdom Collection), trans. Joan M. Burnham (San Rafael, CA: New World Library, 1992), p. 17.

2. C. S. Lewis, *The Silver Chair* (New York: Collier Books, 1970), p. 159.

3. Joel Green, *The Gospel of Luke* (Grand Rapids, MI: William B. Eerdmans Publishing Company, 1997), p. 779.

4. Benedicta Ward, *The Sayings of the Desert Fathers* (Kalamazoo, MI: Cistercian Publications, 1984), pp. 219-220.

5. Raymond E. Brown, *The Anchor Bible: The Gospel According to John XIII-XXI* (Garden City, NY: Doubleday and Company, Inc., 1970), p. 869.

6. Ibid., p. 919.

7. C. S. Lewis, *The Lion, the Witch and the Wardrobe* (New York: Collier Books, 1970), p. 180.

8. "Wouldn't It Be Loverly?" Lyrics by Alan Jay Lerner. Music by Frederick Loewe. © 1956 (Renewed) by Alan Jay Lerner and Frederick Loewe. Publication and allied rights assigned to Chappell and Company. All rights reserved, including public performance for profit. Used by permission.

9. Thanks to Tracie Bullis for suggesting the connection between God's life-giving breath and Jesus' last breath.

10. Donald Hagner, *Word Biblical Commentary: Matthew 12–28*, vol. 33b (Dallas, TX: Word Incorporated, 1995), p. 864.

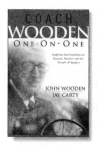
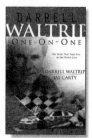